GOD MUST HAVE
FORGOTTEN ABOUT ME

JASON LEE

HOUSE CAPACITY PUBLISHING LLC
DETROIT

House Capacity Publishing
Kierra@housecapacity.com
www.housecapacity.com

Printed in the United States of America

ISBN-13: 978-0-578-61457-1
ISBN-10: 057861457X

For Rodney

CONTENTS

ACKNOWLEDGMENTS

I submit this book to the world with all of the pain, love, promises, and fears that I've endured. I've planned a lot of things, but authorship was not one. But as I've looked back over my life thus far, I knew I had to share my journey with the world.

Getting here hasn't been by chance or luck. First and foremost, I thank God because he gave me the strength to endure and the clarity to see it was my purpose to share.

To the Easter Family: thank you for showing me God and allowing me to become a part of your family. You helped shape the MAN I've become. To Pastor Easter and Elnora Easter: I know I never told you both that I loved you, but I did and still do.

To my sister, Tamica Barney: we've been through a lot and we have a lot more to go. You have always been my biggest supporter, and that means a lot. Thank you for always being there.

To my cousin, Anthony Dunn. You've been an unconditional staple of my inner circle. Love and appreciate you.

Thank you, Kitchie, for the introduction to Floyd Mayweather. Who would have thought we would become family.

To Floyd, you have undoubtedly instilled a passion in me that can not be measured. You have been more than a man of your word. You have been such a generous light to so many people, and I would have never found the courage to start Hollywood Unlocked had you not told me I had a big future. Thank you for being my family.

To Calvin Phillips, my best friend: thank you for holding me the night Rodney died and for never wavering on our friendship. You have always been my ace, and I know God put you in my life to keep me balanced.

To Lature Van Duren: thanks for showing me that I could love and trust someone. I know I drive you crazy, but as you know, I blame you lol. You're an amazing soul. Please stay true to who you are and never leave.

To Edwin Fleming: I wish I would have said goodbye. Thanks for making me feel special when it seemed like nobody wanted me.

To Dana A.K.A. Queen Latifah: I don't think I've ever seen you truly receive my words on how impactful you've been on my life. Not because you didn't want to but because you're so humble that I don't think you know how. I love you for what you represent and for always being a light when I needed it. You're a special person and I pray that others get to have someone like you in their lives.

To Kierra James and the staff at House Capacity Publishing LLC, I want to give a special thank you for helping me share my story with the world.

To Jenifer Lewis: after reading your book and having you on my show I knew I needed to put my pain to paper. What a healing experience. Thanks for having the courage to tell your story because in doing so you gave me the courage to tell my own.

To all of the group home staff, teachers, former employers, bus drivers, neighbors, union members, friends and family that helped shape who I've become I thank you. I don't regret anything because it's all led me to this place.

JASON LEE UNLOCKED

I REMEMBER SITTING WITH MY ACCOUNTANT and going through all the money that I've made throughout my career. Reality TV money, consulting money, event-hosting money—I realized that I didn't enjoy it. None of it. I'm grateful for what I have, and I can honestly say that I've done well for myself: I started my own company, I'm on the cast of "Wild 'N Out," I'm on "Love & Hip Hop," and I have a syndicated radio show that is live in 52 markets. I became partners with Floyd Mayweather, one of the richest athletes in the world, and I've befriended some of the most talented, notable people in the entertainment industry. I know everybody, but not everybody knows me. They know Hollywood Unlocked. They know how I act a fool on "Wild 'N Out." They know some of the dramatic situations I've been a part of on "Love & Hip Hop." They know my industry beefs and my clap-backs. They know what's on my Instagram.

And since I've mentioned Instagram, if you go through my page, you won't see pictures of anyone who I'm in an intimate relationship with. You don't see my family. You don't see anything personal. People don't know me. People know what I've given them, and I've given them my work. I've given them my brand. I've given them exactly what I wanted them to have.

This is the first opportunity I've given people to actually know me. I'm unlocked, and this is my storyline in front of the whole world. My narrative. No coaching, no filter, no holding back. I'm excited to present something that shows who I am. I think when people read this, their perspective will shift, although I didn't write this to convince or beg people to see me a certain way; I don't really care about that. I've made my money the best way I knew how, but I guess as with most people, I'm looking to be understood. I'm looking for people to connect with me. I'm not just the blogger who starts shit, the blogger who shows up and drops the tea, or the blogger who's got the plug on everything. I tell the truth. The truth hurts people sometimes, but I want people to really understand my truth and my journey.

In this book, I'm introducing you to broken Jason. The bright seven-year-old boy who had his light dimmed with the reality and cruelty of his circumstances. The rebellious 10-year-old boy who fought like hell to make it in the foster care system. The angry, fragile Jason who had to figure out how to live after experiencing debilitating trauma. The determined Jason who tapped into his inner anguish and used it as fuel to propel himself in the entertainment industry.

My story is for people of color. It's for white people. It's for young teens as well as seasoned adults. It's for mothers, fathers, grandparents, sisters, brothers—family. It's especially relevant to anybody who is following a dream, anybody who was abandoned by his or her family, anybody who had or currently has parents on drugs or who is the product of a single-parent household. I'm also reaching out to people who have been victims of abuse, and anyone who's trying to figure out how to persevere or overcome trauma. This book is for those who feel stuck or lost. Those who are going through the hardest trials of their lives.

This book is probably the most important book I'm ever going to write. I've told a lot of my stories about my background on my show, but this is an opportunity for me to search myself and share details of my experiences. Here is a way for me to illustrate and provide color and texture to my feelings and emotions. I am certain that my story will impact other people because, shit, I went through too much for it not to help someone else. I also know how powerful words are, and I believe in the power of testimony.

1

SURVIVING STOCKTON

'LL NEVER FORGET THE first time I saw someone get killed. Even though I was only seven years old, I was able to walk to the store by myself—the store, although it was like two or three blocks away, was in the roughest part of town. One time while I was headed there, two guys got into an argument out front. One of the guys nonchalantly pulled out a knife and started stabbing the other guy in the neck. He didn't care who else was in the store or who else had seen him. He was literally sawing his fucking neck like a piece of wood. Blood was squirting everywhere.

I was as white as a fucking Klan sheet, but I still ran in to get some milk. I rushed back out, but I couldn't shake the memory of this man bleeding out and dying in the store. In broad daylight. A motherfucker just sawed someone's head off. Surviving Stockton was a miracle. I had chance against me. I needed to do whatever I could to not only survive Stockton, but to become everything great that my environment wouldn't allow.

***

I grew up on Sutter Street in Stockton, California. We lived in a two-bedroom apartment: my sister, my mom, and me. It was well furnished and we lived comfortably—at least to my standard. But now, looking back, I realize that we lived in a rough part of the city. It's *rough*, rough now, but it wasn't as rough in the early '80s...even with crack being pushed into our neighborhood. I wouldn't say we were poor, but we weren't middle class either. I don't really know what we were, but when times were good, we didn't need anything.

My mother was Italian and Greek. She was born and raised in Los Angeles, and then she migrated to Stockton with her family. My father is from Mississippi and migrated to Stockton with his mother and all 14 of his brothers and sisters. I wish I could make up some bullshit about how my mother and father met, fell in love, and started a family together, but the circumstances of my birth weren't that at all. My father was married to another woman when I was born. Shit, he's still married to her.

He had a side relationship with my mother, and she got pregnant. She was a white woman, and in the '70s, the whole idea of having a Black man's baby was already taboo. Not to mention, my mom's mother was racist. I really think my grandmother resented my mother for having a Black child, or it could have been the fact that my mother was raped by her own father. She said she told my grandmother, and she didn't believe her. Needless to say, that was a strained relationship.

My mother's doctor told her to abort me because the child she was pregnant with before me had been born with Down Syndrome and died. Also, my mother had been bitten by a bat so there was speculation that she may have had some poison or some shit that would cause severe complications with me. They wanted her to abort me, but she didn't. That was one of the few things that I thanked my mother for: she gave me a chance to be.

I wasn't the only child my father had on his wife; in fact, he had seven kids out of wedlock. He used to frequent a club called "The Flamingo," along with all the other women he'd fucked and impregnated. I know that he and my mother had been there together at some point because all the women had conflicts with her and with each other. They also made it a point to try to keep my father's children separated.

I don't think my mother and Joann, my father's wife, ever had any direct conflict, but Joann sure as hell didn't fuck with me. When I stayed with my dad after my mom and I started to clash, it was clear that Joann didn't like me at first. I think there was a lot of animosity that she had toward my mom and dad for having a kid out of wedlock, but her ass was the one still married to my dad after he cheated on her multiple times. I digress.

I didn't really spend too much time around Joann; shit, I barely spent time around my father. My oldest brother, Rodney was more of a father figure to me than my dad ever was or could be.

***

Things were good at home until I was about six years old. I loved going to school. I had a big imagination for what school would teach me, and I had the best times playing with other kids. I was in first grade, and I had a girlfriend named Tamara—a white girl with red hair and freckles. It was ironic because my sister, Tamica, was a big fan of Strawberry Shortcake, and Tamara reminded me of Strawberry Shortcake in a lot of ways. Back in those days, I was a bright, whimsical curly-haired kid, and there were a few girls who thought I was cute. I didn't pay them any mind because my heart belonged to Tamara, and I was going to be faithful to her, damn it. I decided to take the next big step in our relationship, so I gathered up the courage to talk to Tamara about it.

"Tamara, you're pretty," I declared. "I think we should hold hands when we go to the playground."

She looked at me curiously. "But if I hold your hand, how will I jump rope?"

She got me. I hadn't thought that far into our blissful future. "Hmm," I calculated. "Why don't we just hold hands when we go out on the playground and then we let go?"

She was down with this idea. So, for a few days, we would go out, hand in hand, living in a first-grade romance.

I loved school and looked forward to helping my teacher do things around the classroom. Whenever she would need help passing out supplies, I shot up like a bullet to be the first volunteer. Her response to me was always warm and encouraging, and I looked forward to her approving smiles each day. I loved learning, and math was my favorite subject. Even though we were doing simple math, it was rewarding to figure out a puzzle of numbers and symbols and be celebrated for having the right answer.

***

"Put your hands up!" I burst through the door after another day of school. I would take the bus home, so after I reached my stop, I would go straight home.

"Oh, you got me!" my mother would giggle and play along. I wanted to be a police officer when I grew up, so I was everyone's tiny-tot deputy for a while. Both my mom and dad were correction officers, and it was fun to hear stories about the things that would happen at the prison where they worked. I loved seeing my mother in her uniform even though she wasn't quite a police officer. I was a kid, so shit, she was the police to me.

I lowered my weapon and then scanned the area for my favorite beverage: "Mom, do we have any more chocolate milk?" I was a fiend for chocolate back then. Shit, even today if you really want to make me happy, drizzle a little chocolate on something and we're good.

"Let me check, baby. I think your sister might have drunk the last one."

I immediately shot a threatening look at Tamica, who was only about three years old at the time. I'm sure she didn't notice or care that I was upset about her drinking the milk.

"Aha! I found one!" I all but wagged my tail when my mother produced that little brown and white box of chocolatey pleasure. I was living the life. What's there to live for if a man can't come home from school to a cold box of chocolate milk and then watch some cartoons in his Superman pajamas?

***

I loved my mom then, and she was a good mother before the drugs. She was very loving and nurturing, and she did a lot for us, even though she was a single mother. I think she was very proud to have her kids during those days. When she was in a good mood, she would fill the house with the sounds of Michael Jackson or Prince, or some R&B and Marvin Gaye. I would look on bashfully as she sang and twirled to the music.

"C'mon! Dance, Jason!"

I couldn't pass up on the invitation. As a kid, I loved to dance, and Michael Jackson was my favorite entertainer. At her beckoning, I burst into a moonwalk, twirled, and then grabbed my crotch. She was eating it up. I only had an audience of one, but I was killing it like I was on stage at Madison Square Garden.

Christmas used to be good for us. My mom would have Santa come over, and we got every toy we wanted. One of my favorite gifts was a pogo stick. I used to hop all over the parking lot with that thing; we weren't allowed to play anywhere else because our neighborhood was so bad. For birthdays, our parties were always the shit. All the community kids would come over, and we would have fun. Like normal kids, we dressed up for Halloween and went trick-or-treating. Those were the days when she was present.

When my mother got into drugs, a lot changed. She wasn't abusive; she was just more absent. She left us home alone often, and my sister and I had to take care of ourselves. Then we got babysitters, but that didn't last long. I was three years older than my sister, Tamica, but I was the person who used to meet Tamica after school. I was her caregiver at seven years old—I made sure she ate and bathed, and even tried my hand at potty training:

"I pee-peed!" she would shriek.

"Ok, let me find the diapers." I located a chair so I could stand and look on the top shelf where my mother usually kept them. I procured one, but it took me more than a few times before I was able to figure it out.

"Ok, here's a new diaper, but you gotta use the toilet the next time, ok?"

"Okay, Jason!"

I would help her with her homework, and we would play school at home. I would also pretend to be a teacher— she'd be my student, and I'd go over her homework. Tamica was only in preschool, so she didn't really have homework, but we used to pretend that she did.

"Hey, Tamica, what starts with A?"

She thought for a second and then she lit up, confident that she had figured it out.

"Fruit Loops!"

Total facepalm. "No, no. A makes the 'aah' sound. Try it again."

"Apple!"

"That's right!" I encouraged. "You're so smart!"

I could see her basking in all my affirmations.

Tamica's father wasn't really in the picture, but when he would come around, he made disgusting comments about my relationship with Tamica. I heard him tell my mother that he suspected I was molesting her and that we were having a sexual relationship. We were kids! Who would think that? He had no idea that no one else was taking care of Tamica but me. Or maybe he did know; my mother's drug use wasn't exactly a secret. If he was so concerned about her well-being he could have acted like an actual father and taken care of her himself.

***

My mother's absentee parenting style turned me into a grown ass man. I had a key around my neck that I would use to get in and out of the apartment whenever I desired. I would wake up on my own, get ready for school, and walk to the bus stop by myself. No one at school suspected anything because I was there every day and on time. My mom was out running the streets, and I would get into trouble—normal shit kids would do. I would get my sister to throw mud on our building manager's windows and on the wall, or we'd knock on people's doors and run.

At seven years old, I was a latchkey kid, but because my mom was using all her money to buy drugs, there wasn't enough money to pay for latchkey or any of our basic essentials. There was a kid who lived in my building who had a peculiar way of making money, and he told me to come with him to a funeral home that was nearby. That was the strangest request, but I was just like, "Fuck it, ok." When we got there, there was a viewing going on, and we had sat among the grieving family members. I wondered if this was some-body he knew because he didn't really say much while we were there. We waited for about an hour, and finally people were starting to leave and the room was emptying out. He looked around at first but then he walked up to the casket, unhooked the chain that was on the body, and then put it in his pocket. He motioned for me to follow him and then we left.

"Oh my God! You stole the chain!" I was so confused and shocked at the same time. He laughed and told me to follow him to an area where a bunch of guys were hanging out on a stoop.

"Whatchu got for us today, lil' nigga?" one of the guys asked.

The kid pulled the chain out his pocket and presented it to the group.

"I think it's 14 karat gold, and there aren't any scratches or spots anywhere." He was selling them all the features of the chain like he worked for the fucking Home Shopping Network.

"Aight, cool. How much you want for it?" I guess his little sales pitch worked.

"$50."

"Hell nah! I'll give you $30."

They both agreed on the price, and when we walked back to the building, I had all the questions.

"So, you just steal stuff from dead people and sell them?"

"Yes."

"And you never got caught?"

"No. That's stupid. If I got caught, I wouldn't go back."

I smiled and the proverbial light bulb went off in my head. I had found a way to solve our money problem. The next time he went to the funeral home, I was right there with him. We had found all kinds of rings, chains, and watches and were making pretty good money. Sometimes I went by myself if he couldn't go. I had earned enough money to pay for latchkey and to buy groceries. I bought all kinds of crazy shit that a seven-year-old would buy: pies, cookies, juice, cereal—nothing of nutritional value, but we didn't starve. By this time, we were also on government assistance and were receiving paper food stamps and WIC. Government cheese was the shit. I would stay outside walking the neighborhood until at least 9 pm. Normal seven-year-olds would have been tucked into bed already, but I was just doing me. I would walk past the local drug dealers and gang-bangers on the regular, and even they thought it was peculiar for me to be out by myself and at that time of night.

"What's good, D-Rock?" I tried my hardest to put a little bass in my voice to turn down my naturally high-pitched squeal. Gotta be gangsta if you're going to approach the ganstas, you know?

"Haha! Wassup my lil' nigga!" he slapped my hand like I was one of the guys. "Whatcho lil' ass out here doing?"

"Chillin."

The whole gang of Bloods burst out laughing. "I feel that shit," D-Rock chuckled. "Where yo mama at?"

I dropped my gaze. I didn't know where she was, but I knew what she was probably doing. What was most embarrassing is that I knew they knew, too. They were probably the ones who sold her the drugs in the first place.

"I'll holler at cha'll later. I'm bouta check on my sister." I raised my hand for some more "dap."

"Aight," one of the other guys responded. "Aye, lil' nigga, get you some chips, or some juice, or some shit." He had reached in his pocket and gave me five dollars. It was funny because I already had about $100 in my pocket from selling jewelry, but I took the money anyway.

"Thanks," I nodded up.

***

The whole neighborhood knew who I was because I was always walking around unattended. I was comfortable; in my eyes, it wasn't as bad as people made it out to be—but it was. One day, I went to a little pop-up carnival beside a gas station not too far from our house—maybe six or seven blocks. I walked to the carnival and some guy asked me to go into the bathroom with him. I didn't think much of it so I went. Once I got inside, a sinister grin spread across his face and he whipped his dick out. He started rubbing and stroking it—first gently until he was fully erect. Then he masturbated in front of me. He didn't touch me or anything like that, but it was still molestation.

I ran home to tell my mother, but it was hard for her to believe me. I was pissed because she acted like I was making it all up. That was crazy to me because she was molested by her own father and her mother didn't believe her. She knew exactly what it felt like to be called a liar in the face of such a confession. Finally, I convinced her to do something about it, and she took me to the police station. We filed a report and the police said that they'd be on the lookout for the guy. *That's it?* Police officers were supposed to be heroes and protect everyone from bad guys. I mean, that's why I wanted to be one. They'd done nothing and I found myself contemplating at seven years old if law enforcement was for me.

But that wasn't the last time a man would violate me.

My mother started the search again for another babysitter. This time, she decided on a family friend, a girl who was probably in her mid-twenties. She would drop Tamica and me off at Jeanette's house, and every time we were there, her boyfriend was, too. I don't remember his name; I just know that he was Latino and that he had a son who was a little younger than me. Jeanette and Tamica must have been preoccupied or gone because he called me into the room one morning and told me to close the door.

"Come here, Jason," he called to me. He was fully naked, and he had an erect penis. I don't know why I came over to him, but

I did reluctantly. He told me to take my clothes off and to get on top of him. I did. He started grinding on me while we were under the blanket. This happened a few times when I would go over Jeanette's house. Sometimes he asked me to touch his penis, but he never penetrated me or asked for oral sex. Of course, I didn't tell anybody because I didn't even know who to tell or how to tell. The first time I told my mom about the guy in the bathroom at the carnival, she didn't believe me.

Though what he did to me was deplorable, it started a journey of discovery about my sexuality. There are people who believe that people are born gay or that being gay is a choice; I can say that I don't ever remember having gay feelings before the molestation. It was a weird rush of feelings because, on one end, I didn't enjoy what he was doing to me, but on the other end, I was aroused. I was in a weird space. This wasn't the same flutters I felt when I held hands with Strawberry Shortcake Tamara, this was something different—and confusing. I didn't know gay or straight. My mom even had a friend who was transsexual, and I didn't even know what that was. I eventually became numb to the experiences with Jeanette's boyfriend, but I was curious about myself as a sexual being.

***

By the second grade, I had turned into a completely different kid in school. I was rebellious and uncooperative. I was constantly sent to the principal's office, and when he would ask me what was wrong, I'd just say, "Nothing." We were taught not to tell our business. It was an exact demonstration of the old Black adage, "What goes on in this house stays in this house." I couldn't tell him that I was having sexual experiences with my babysitter's boyfriend or that my mom was on crack. In so many ways, I was screaming for help, but it felt like nobody could hear me.

My mom's drug addiction started to get worse, and she started to get heavy into cocaine and heroin. Once she became a heroin addict, she became a prostitute. Because she was no longer paying any bills, we ended up getting evicted and moving into a motel. One time, I was coming back to the room with one of my friends, and I saw my mom in bed with one of her clients. We disrupted her time with him, so she leaped up, grabbed a belt and smacked me on the back.

"Ow!" I squealed. "Why are you hitting me?" She grabbed me and took me in the bathroom and let me have it some more. I was screaming, snotting, and crying, but she was unmoved.

"You're causing too many fucking problems, you know that?" she slapped me with the belt a few more times.

I didn't understand how coming home was a problem. We lived in a motel in one wide-open space. There was no privacy for her to be bringing clients there.

She yelled at me, and once she calmed down, she said, "That's it. You have to go." I think things became too much for her to deal with. I told her about Jeanette's boyfriend a few weeks before, and she blamed me for getting molested. At the same time, I think she was feeling guilty for not watching me. On top of that, she still wanted to be a prostitute to survive, and she was still addicted to heroin. She called Child Protective Services, and they were knocking on our door within the hour. A frail white woman came inside and spoke to my mother. She was using a lot of jargon like "custody," and "parental rights"; I didn't know what it meant, but I felt uneasy about the conversation. The woman then directed her attention toward me.

"Is this Jason?" she asked my mother.

"Yes," she confirmed. She didn't even look at me when she said it. She maintained an aloof disposition and I wondered why I'd felt so eerie.

"Hi, Jason, I'm Mrs. Brogue," she began. "How are you?"

"Good," I replied, skeptical. I was still broken from my mother's ass-whooping, but I wasn't going to tell that lady about it. I looked back at my mother and she completely withdrew from the conversation.

"I'm a social worker; do you know what that is?"

"No," I answered. Mrs. Brogue was stalling, and I could tell. I didn't know why she was here, but I knew it wasn't good.

"A social worker is a person who helps make sure that all children live in a safe home and that they have what they need. Sometimes that's not easy for every parent to do, so we work to get you into a home that's better equipped to help with that."

"But I already have a home," I challenged her.

"Yes, you do!" she smiled. "However, your mom told us that she might need a little time to make sure that you have an even better home and that she can work on being a better mom to you, too."

I was confused. I didn't know what she was trying to tell me, but by then, my mom had gone to the bathroom and didn't come back out again.

"You're going to come with me, and I'm going to take you to a home where—"

"But I don't want to go to another home," I trembled. "I have a home!"

"I understand that, but we want to make sure that you—"

"Mom!" I yelled at the bathroom door. "She wants to take me!" My mother stayed inside and didn't respond. "Mom!"

"I'm sorry, Jason, I didn't mean to upset you," Mrs. Brogue attempted to calm the situation, "but I promise that we won't hurt you and that you will be ok."

"MOM!" I screamed again. Her silence made me burst out into tears and I just collapsed onto the floor. "Mom, I'm sorry!" I pleaded at the door. "I don't want to go!"

By this time, a man had come in and stood beside Mrs. Brogue. I saw him, and I knew that he was going to help her take me. I also knew that I wouldn't be able to get away from him. I wailed all the way to the small van, and I constantly looked back at the raggedy hotel hoping that my mother would emerge and change her mind.

My mother sent me with the social worker and sent Tamica to live with her father; that began my animosity toward her. They took me away, and shortly after, I was immersed in the foster care system. I didn't understand how she was able to let them take me. I no longer recognized who my mother was. Drugs had completely taken over her life, and from that moment on, our relationship was never the same.

2

FOSTER CARE

M Y FIRST NIGHT IN FOSTER CARE was at a place called Mary Graham
Children's Shelter. I came from a house that felt like a home, with
a mother and a sister, to a building with 50-100 kids. I can't remember how many kids were there, but there were plenty of staff coming
into our rooms to check on us all the time. I was there with a roommate that I didn't know, and the whole experience was lonely and
confusing. I didn't understand why I was there or when I was going
to be able to leave. I didn't know anybody, and I was being taken care
of by a bunch of strangers. It was very weird.

On one side of the building were all guys; the girls were on the
other side. There was a desk in the middle where the staff sat and
monitored everyone who was in the building. We would have TV

time and then recreational time; afterward, we would eat meals together. The staff would even take us to school, which was weird to me because I had always been responsible for taking myself.

I started rebelling quickly. One night, I just felt like I didn't want to be there so I thought, *Maybe if I just act out, these people will kick me out.* I didn't know they had rooms where they would restrain kids who thought just like I did. The room reminded me of all the movies I watched when a person was in a room in a mental hospital—you know, white padded walls and a straitjacket. They didn't have straitjackets at Mary Graham's, but they had methods to prevent a kid from going in there and hurting himself. Some kids would act a fool in there, so everyone was always monitored closely.

In my rebellion, I did mischievous things—luckily, I never ended up in that goddamn room. One of my roommates had a big jar of marbles, and one particular night, I waited until midnight, and I got out of bed. I crept over to the area where my roommate kept the marbles, and I threw the whole bucket of marbles down the hallway. Mind you, it was really quiet. Everybody was in bed sleeping except my little ass, and then all of a sudden, here came all these marbles crashing down the hallway. I acted like I was asleep, and everybody thought my roommate had thrown the bucket of marbles because they were his. He got in trouble for it, but I kept doing shit like that.

I started getting into fights early on. I don't remember ever being violent or wanting to fight before, but I quickly realized that I would have to learn how to survive in that place. I always stayed ready to throw some hands—that came out of my decision to stand my ground with people and not let them think that they could take advantage of me. I was afraid, but I could never let that fear show.

Not long after I entered Mary Graham's, I was being prepped for my first foster home. Steven, one of the social workers, sat with me and told me about the Chapman family and how the process worked. I was so afraid. I was going to be living in a house with strangers; how was this going to be better for me than living with my own mother? Steven also told me that my stay with the Chapmans would be temporary—although he had no idea how long my stay would be. I prepared myself for another major transition and remained hopeful that this nightmare would end and that my mother would come and rescue me.

The Chapmans were a seemingly religious Black family. I think my foster dad was a firefighter—I wasn't 100% sure. What I am sure about is the fact that he was abusive to the foster kids. He would whoop everybody. Our social worker would always tell us that our foster parents weren't allowed to hit us because we were wards of the state, but Mr. Chapman didn't give a fuck. We used to be bad, but he whooped us like he *wanted* the state to know about it.

Eventually, I didn't last long with the Chapmans, and I ended up back at Mary Graham's Children's Shelter. I befriended a lot of the staff there: Ms. Tisdale, Ms.Hodge, and Ms. Thomlinson to name a few. They really liked me because I was always dancing, and I was this little cute kid who was full of personality. I was only like eight or nine, but I had a big mouth, and I would always talk shit.

Entertaining the staff helped me cope with being away from my mom, and it helped me stuff down the feelings I had after being molested.

Even though I would laugh and joke while at Mary Graham's, my mission was clear: get back home. I managed to slip away one day while we were at an outing with some staff members. I tried to make it back to the hotel where my mother was, but someone found me before I was even a few blocks away. *Damn.* I was reprimanded for trying to leave, but I didn't care. The loss of a few privileges meant nothing to me. I knew that I didn't belong there and I was going to fight like hell to get out.

***

I left Mary Graham's again and went to another foster home. I became closer to the Easters more so than any other family during my entire time in the system. Mr. Easter was a pastor, and his wife was the first lady of the church. They had four sons and three daughters—I was really close to two of their daughters and three of their sons. They also had grandkids who were like my siblings and cousins because they were closer to my age. I went to school with them and we did all kinds of activities together, too. This was the first time I'd actually felt like I had a family—more so than my own.

When I first got there, I was a little fucking terror. One summer afternoon I was in the backyard, and I noticed that they had a big fire extinguisher hanging up by the back porch. I snatched it, sprayed it everywhere, and yelled, "Fire!" Thick white smoke took over the backyard. Mrs. Easter thought that I had lit the house on fire, so she screamed and ran to get her husband. It was a prank. I ended up getting a whooping by Pam, one of Mr. and Mrs. Easter's daughters, and I immediately hated Pam because she brought back all the feelings and reminders of abuse I'd experienced before. Eventually, I worked through them, but I was done with Pam for a long time. She had physically disciplined me, and she knew she wasn't supposed to.

The Easters introduced me to Christianity and becoming a Pentecostal. My mother was Catholic, and she used to take me to Mass for Ash Wednesday and all that kind of stuff, but I didn't really identify with that. I mean, I went because she wanted me to go to church, but it wasn't something that I actually connected with. When I was with the Easters, we were in church all the time— like literally every single day: choir practice, usher board meeting, fucking Sunday school, Bible study, prayer, and whatever other random services and revivals that popped up. As much as I complained, I appreciated it because I was learning about the Bible. I was learning the books of the Bible, and more about God. That's when I first started to develop my faith.

I never had a father figure, but Pastor Easter stepped in not only as a natural father but also as a spiritual father. I was struggling with the relationship with my mom, I had lost the relationship with my sister, and I had no relationship with my dad, but Pastor Easter taught me the importance of having a relationship with God. The way he talked about God was hard for me to understand because I didn't believe God would allow all these negative things to happen to a kid. I thought God must have forgotten about me. Pastor Easter reassured me that God had not forgotten and that it would be only a matter of time before I saw God's hand in my life even through my tribulations.

Above all, Pastor Easter was very positive, very active, and very present. I was able to see how, not only his wife honored him, but also how his kids honored him. At first, I was confused because I didn't understand why they would esteem him so highly. My father was the complete opposite of Pastor Easter. While my father acted like I didn't exist most of the time, Pastor Easter was very caring. He provided for the family. He was that guy who worked and brought home the money.

Mrs. Elnora Easter was just as wonderful. She was loving, caring, positive, and always praying with or for others. The first time I had ever eaten soul food was with the Easters, and I fell in love with her peach cobbler from then on. One time, I just mentioned in passing how much I was craving peach cobbler, and the next thing I knew, she was gathering ingredients and rolling out dough. Slowly, the scent of cinnamon, brown sugar, and vanilla began to saturate the house.

"What are you doing?" I questioned her. I just knew she didn't stop what she was doing just to bake a cobbler for me.

"What do you think?" she smiled. "We have not because we ask not. You asked, baby."

I had never known anyone to regard me in that way, but that's who she was. She was thoughtful and attentive. She wasn't just a Christian in word, she lived it every day. She was that kind of person.

I also appreciated Mrs. Easter because I could always talk to her about my mom. She was very motherly, but she never tried to replace my mother. Even when I told her the most abhorrent things about my mom, she always encouraged me to be positive and to pray for my mother. She never disrespected my mom or judged her for the decisions she had made; she tried to help me understand, the best she could, what my mother was going through. It's because of Mrs. Easter that I even tried to have a relationship with my mom despite all she had done. I clung to Mrs. Easter's advice to always honor her and to forgive her—but later in life, that became increasingly harder to do.

***

I loved the Easters. They really instilled faith in God and discipline. They gave me hope that things could get better. They were a lovely couple, but no matter how hard I tried, I couldn't completely be happy there. I still felt the sting of rejection, and, as crazy as it sounds, I missed my mother. I felt like my place was with her, and despite all the love and care I received from the Easters, I needed to get back to where I belonged. As I started getting closer to them, I started feeling like my relationship with my mom was fading.

My solution was to find my mom. Every time I went somewhere, I was always trying to run away to get back to her. One time, I was supposed to go to church, but I didn't want to go. I swear, the only form of abuse I experienced with the Easters was being forced to attend all the church services they had. I needed a break. I ended up staying home, and they locked me in the house. I broke out and snuck out to go meet with my mom. When I came to her motel, she was shooting up heroin. I had convinced a buddy to come with me to find my mother, and when I found her, she didn't even try to hide what she was doing. She shot up right in front of me and my friend.

"Mom! Why are you doing that?" I cried. She had a glazed-over look in her eyes like she didn't even know I was there. Maybe she thought that I was just a hallucination. She didn't seem happy to see me and she didn't ask anything about my new family. I became angry at her for her disregard. "Look at you! Stop! I pray for you, Mrs. Easter prays for you, and you don't even care!" Still, nothing.

She ended up passing out with the needle in her arm. I just sat on the edge of the bed crying. I didn't want to leave her like that, but I didn't want to stay because I didn't know if she was expecting someone who wouldn't be too happy to see me there. I knew how much trouble I would be in for running away, and so, I resolved to stay until she woke up.

"Jason, what are you doing here?" she shrieked.

"Mom, I just want to be with you!" I answered. "I'll stay and help you get better. Mrs. Easter said that God is working on you."

In a real gargly raspy voice she said, "What the fuck does Mrs. Easter know about what God is doing to me?"

I was speechless. I thought that all my praying was working, but it wasn't.

"I'm going to call Mary Grahams and get you and your friend back to where you came from."

"No!" I sobbed. "I'm your son; you're supposed to take care of me!"

She and my friend both looked at me like I had a finger growing out of my ear.

"I can't take care of you," she proclaimed. As she said, she called the people at Mary Graham's to pick us up. They came and took us back. I didn't understand. I was so confused about that. Why didn't she want me?

I didn't realize that my mother knew I was with the Easters and that she was actually communicating with them to make sure that I had a safe place to live. She hadn't completely abandoned me; I guess she was still looking out for me.

***

I had done some other mischievous things while I was with the Easters, but after I had run away, that was the final straw. As much as they loved and cared about me, they realized that I was troubled and would probably fare better in an environment that had the tools to help me manage my issues. I had been with the Easters for about a year and a half before I was sent to a new facility.

I never kept in touch with anybody from the Mary Graham Children's Shelter or the Chapmans, but I always kept in touch with the Easters. I would still go to their church. Their church was where I was baptized. Their church is where I was saved. Their church is where I was in the choir, and where my friends were. That church was important to me, so I'd always keep going. Even when I went back home with my family and with my mom, I'd still go back to that church. They were still a part of my family. They went out of their way to make me feel loved, and I hadn't felt that in a while. As much as I enjoyed my time with the Easters, I was still very numb about leaving them. I was groomed to pick up the pieces and keep it moving, not to sit and sulk. I missed them, and, of course, I missed the situation, but I didn't believe that life went in reverse, so I wasn't going back.

***

I was on the move again, and this time I was sent to a group home called The Children's Home of Stockton. It was like Mary Graham's Children's Shelter but smaller—probably like eight guys on the unit. At Mary Graham's, we went to school on site, but here we also had the option to go to public school. We had more activities here, and we had chores. We would help cook dinner, and we had counseling.

School at the Children's Home was ok. The kids weren't really bad, and we actually had a decent curriculum. There was a lot of focus on arts and technology, and they allowed us to explore our own interests and passions. The class size was small enough so that nobody got left behind. Now that I think about it, it probably was the best educational opportunity I had.

School was tame, but it was the house that was crazy. Fights would break out all the time, and I could feel my soul grow dimmer by the day. I didn't belong there. All I wanted to do was go back home.

***

I was pissed at the system. They kept moving me around, and everybody expected me to be perfect when I wasn't. They expected me to behave like a normal kid and they had the nerve to be fucking surprised when I would lash out. I was a kid who ran the streets at seven years old. Instead of talking to family members and mentors, I kicked it with drug dealers. I'd seen people get murdered, and my mother was strung out on drugs and prostituting to make ends meet. I grew up really fast. I was used to coming home at like 9:00 pm. No other seven-year-olds were doing that, and there was no goddamn reason why they should have been. On top of it all, I was a child who experienced sexual trauma. Shit, how was I supposed to act?

To me, I was grown before I left my mom, and I was grown afterward. I was going into foster care and all these group homes, and I had people constantly telling me what to do. I didn't understand having to go to bed at like 7:00 or 8:00. *What are you talking about?* When I came to the Children's Home, that's when I really started losing faith in "the system" because it felt like a system. You act out here, you're going to get kicked out. You can push boundaries at certain levels, and they can't hit you. If you get somewhere you don't like, you can run away. I was institutionalized, and I lost a sense of what family was. No one in my family tried to find me, and no one came to rescue me like I had hoped. I didn't remember much about my dad; he wasn't around at all during this period of my life. He never came to see me when I was in foster care, even though we were all in the same city.

***

My mom eventually came to see me. She brought Tamica to the children's home where I was staying at the time. We had a good meeting, and she said she was doing better.

"Can I leave?" I looked at her square on and tried not to let my desperation to come home overwhelm me during the visit.

My mom's eyes shifted, and she said, "No."

"Why?" I felt like I was at my wit's end, and that I couldn't hold on any longer.

She told me, "Because I'm not all the way better."

I took a deep breath and let her have it:

"Well, I'm confused about how a mother isn't ready to take care of her own fucking kid. At this point, you're already three years in. Why you ain't better after three years? It's a long time. Why you ain't better at this point?"

She dropped her head and nearly whispered, "I'm doing the best that I can."

That conversation was pivotal. I really got angry with her because I didn't understand how a mother could tell her child, "I love this drug, and I'm choosing this lifestyle over you." At least that's how I interpreted it. "I'm doing the best that I can," wasn't enough. Her best was shitty. I thought that was a cop-out. It wasn't until years later that I understood what she was really saying: this was all that she *could* do. This *was* her best. But as a ten-year-old boy, I couldn't understand that, nor did I have the ability to empathize with her addiction. I had animosity toward her because I was hurt. I went from really loving her and valuing her to wanting to completely destroy her emotionally. I was very mean to her, and I really was looking for retribution. She had gone from being my hero, the one who did everything she could to love and nurture me, to being the main villain in my life. She showed me how it felt to be forgotten and abandoned. She taught me hate and hostility.

Every visitation became repetitive. I knew what was going to happen. She was going to come, she was going to bring me McDonald's, we were going to have a good conversation, and then she was going to leave me there because she wasn't ready. That happened for a long time. I tore into smaller shreds each time she left. At least she came to visit. She did show up. I'll give her that credit.

3

READJUSTING

───────

WHEN I LEFT FOSTER CARE, I was 14 years old. Living with my mother was the only option I had, so there I was, heading back to the person who had shown me that she had no problem choosing everything else but me.

The day of my release, my social worker dropped me off at a big beautiful house on Acacia Street. My mother had moved in with a guy named John, an old Chinese man. He had Samurai swords and nice antiques on display from China. Walking around his house was almost like being in a museum; it was clean and it looked like no one really lived in it.

My mom and I both had our own rooms; mine was in the attic that he used as a library. I don't know the extent of John and my mom's relationship, and I didn't ask. I did notice that she was not the same as she was before I went to foster care. I could tell that she had been through a lot and that life had worn her out. Still, I offered her no warmth and no place in my heart. I didn't know if she desired that from me, but I didn't care if she did. I became very callous toward my mother and was very difficult to deal with.

I was in the streets all the time. One of the biggest points of contention between my mother and me was that she wanted me home, but I wanted to be everywhere else but home. I no longer desired her love or her acceptance, and I resented her for giving me away. When she would ask my whereabouts and try to keep tabs on me, I didn't take her seriously. Did she forget that when I was younger, she left me in the streets? That's what I knew. I went from extreme freedom to an extreme lack of privacy and control, and now I was back home. I wanted my freedom back.

"You ain't nothing but a fucking nigger!" she would yell out to me sometimes. "You're just like your piece of shit father!"

My mom would cuss me out all the time for disregarding her rules and being so disrespectful to her. I didn't care though. I still did me. I would go back and forth with her until I would expel all my energy and leave. I later learned that my mom suffered from bipolar disorder on top of her drug addiction, but back then, I didn't understand all of that. I just thought she was fucking nuts.

***

I didn't really get bullied until I came back from the group homes and I reentered the community. In eighth grade, I was getting bullied by everybody, and I really didn't know how to deal with people in the public like that. I had been going to a predominantly white school in Oakdale, and I had never been in a school with predominantly Black or Mexican kids. I struggled with public school. I didn't want to be around people, and I especially hated being around groups of people doing the same shit. I didn't know how to adjust to being in a public school setting because I was so used to the smaller class sizes and private school feeling I experienced while being in the system. I had to adjust to being around all these fucking kids who had their own issues and their own personalities. Shit was crazy, and it was overwhelming. There was a lot of tension between everybody for whatever reason, but I got a lot of hate early on. I think it was because my mom didn't really have a lot of money, so I didn't have all the coolest clothes.

I felt like I was cute. I had what was considered "good hair" and all that. I was popular for the most part for that, but when it came to how I dressed or the fact that we were poor, I was bullied. MC Hammer was hot back then, and it seemed like everybody in school was wearing the same parachute pants that Hammer had on. He was from the Bay and I was from Stockton, so I appreciated him as an artist. Somehow, I convinced my mom to buy me a few pairs of pants, and I came home so excited to wear them to school the next day.

When I walked into my first class, I didn't get the reaction I was expecting.

"Aye, nigga, what the fuck you got on!" someone yelled out. And then it was followed by an eruption of laughter from the rest of my classmates. I didn't get it; everybody wore these. Why was it such a thing when I had them on? I was taunted throughout the day about my pants, so I resolved that I would go home and burn them all.

The athletes would also pick on me because I was in music class. Music was something that I enjoyed, but because I wasn't playing football or any other sports, I guess they thought I was soft.

"I bet this nigga can't even fight," I heard one of the boys on the football team say to me while I was putting my things in my locker. I stared at him, but I wasn't in the mood for anybody to be fucking with me.

"Hell naw," another one responded. "The nigga just gone put them pants back on and dance!"

They both broke out in a robust laugh, and I slammed my locker and headed back to class. I thought this would be enough for them to leave me alone, but they were following me still laughing and joking.

"Leave me alone," I warned.

"*Leave me alone!*" one of the boys attempted to mimic me. I felt the anger began to brew, and I remembered those times in Mary Grahams when I would have to bust a nigga in his mouth so they knew I wasn't a punk. I knew what time it was. While he was in mid-giggle, I turned around and punched him in the nose. I was getting ready to handle the other boy, but his eyes widened and he ran to get a teacher. *Cool,* I thought. *Now I ain't gotta fight both of them.* We were exchanging blows back and forth until I felt someone grab me and push me against the wall.

Even though I thought I had done enough to prove myself, kids would still pick on me. It was a horrible time. I was always getting into fights and I hated going to school. I didn't really have any friends—everybody else in my class had been friends since elementary school or at least since the beginning of junior high. I had spent all those formative years in foster care, so I didn't develop those types of friendships. The friends I did have were either still in foster care or attending different schools. I felt alone.

By the time I got to high school, I came in with a whole new disposition. *Fuck that,* I thought. *In high school, I'm not getting bullied anymore.* I stayed ready to fight, and even if someone wanted to be my friend, I was so standoffish and aggressive that I deterred anyone from trying.

***

Right before I left The Children's Home of Stockton, there had been a massive school shooting in our community at Cleveland Elementary School. A man named Patrick Purdy, who used to be in the army, drove his car to the school, which had a predominantly Asian population, and blew the car up outside. When the kids ran out, he was on the school yard, and he shot them all with AK-47s. He killed seven people—one teacher and six kids—and shot countless others.

Some of the counselors at the Children's Home came in to talk to us about the details of the shooting and went over a safety plan with us. It's crazy that this happened maybe 20 years ago, yet America is still having a problem dealing with and preventing school shootings presently. Everyone was on edge and we wondered if we would be next.

That school shooting stayed on my mind for a while, and about a year later, while I was getting ready for school, I heard on the radio that Michael Jackson was coming to town, and when he came to Stockton, he met with all the kids at Cleveland Elementary and told them that God was going to protect them. He urged them not to live in fear and to keep coming to school. He wanted to encourage them in the midst of the tragedy. I thought that was special.

Then he went to the hospital and visited all the people who were wounded, paid for everyone's medical bills, and covered the cost of the funerals. He never wanted any accolades or recognition—he was really low-key about it. That was my first sense of what real compassion looked like, and I was mystified by that. I was already a fan, but now I was determined to meet Michael Jackson. When I finally came home, I did research about him and discovered that his company was called MJJ Productions. I found a working number for the company, and I called every day asking to speak to Michael. He wasn't available, obviously, but I left so many messages and I called so much that I established a relationship with his assistant, Evvy. I would call and spark up the most random conversations with her and then our call would conclude with me leaving a message for Michael. I never thought she would actually relay them.

Much to my excitement, Michael Joseph Jackson finally called me.

It was early in the morning. I was asleep, and the two friends who were staying over my house were asleep, too. I was awakened by the phone, and when I answered, there was a lady on the other end asking to speak to me. I was skeptical because she didn't sound familiar, but I told her that it was me. Then a guy got on the phone to reconfirm, and then he told me to hold the line. A couple of seconds later, Michael was on the phone.

Immediately, I knew it was him, but Michael talked a lot differently than how he talked on interviews and on TV. His voice was his voice, and it was definitely him, but his voice was less whimsical and light. Simply put, he sounded like a nigga. I don't know how to define or explain that, but that's how he sounded.

When he got on the phone, he said, "Yo, Jason, what's up?"

I jumped up, and said, "Hello?"

"What's up?"

"Wait, who is this?" Nobody was going to convince me that fucking Michael Jackson was on that phone.

He laughed and said, "You been calling my office every day and you don't know who this is?"

My heart almost jumped into my throat, and I said, "Well, I think I know who it is, but I want to hear you say it."

He paused and said, "This is Michael Jackson."

"For real? Yo!" I went over to my friends and started kicking the shit out of them to wake them up. I told Michael, "Yo, nobody's ever going to believe that you're calling me!"

"Okay, you called me, so what's up?"

I said, "I didn't think you would call back, so I didn't have a plan, but I'm such a big fan! I'm from Stockton and you were here after that school shooting happened. I think it's dope what you did for everyone."

He said, "Yea, I remember that."

"Where are you?" I asked him like we were cool like that.

"I'm in Trump Tower in New York. I'm recording."

I said, "Okay."

Then he changed his tone completely and asked when I was born.

I said, "August 16th, the same day Elvis Presley died."

"There's an aura about you," he began. "I can feel something special. I can feel your aura through the phone."

"Really?"

"Yeah."

I blushed and said, "Well, thank you." I didn't know what aura he was talking about but it meant a lot that Michael Jackson had said something positive about me. Then I asked, "So can I ever come to Neverland?"

He laughed and said, "I don't know. I'm never really there as much, but we'll see." After that, he told me to stay positive and some other nice things. That was the only time I ever talked to him; I never met him and I never got to go to Neverland, but looking back, it was a testament that I was always surrounded by or connected to greatness somehow.

***

When I came home, I had a strong desire to connect with my siblings. I had a lot of them, but I was really hanging tough with my brothers Link, Chris, and Rodney. I would always take the bus to see them, and they made me feel accepted. I thought I didn't care about love or whether anyone else cared about me, but I knew that they filled me up in ways I hadn't been filled in a while. I built an unbreakable bond with them, and my relationship with my brothers was one that I valued above any other relationships. As rough as they were and as questionable their lifestyles were, I was one of them, and we had each others' backs. They were in a gang, but nobody pressured me into being "official." I was never jumped into the gang, but everybody knew I rolled with them. Link and I were from the south side and Rodney was from the west. He was a Louis Park Piru, and both he and Link were about eight years older than me. I would hang with Rodney and Link all the time. Rodney was 6' 5" 230 pounds, and the whole town knew not to fuck with him. When I wasn't with my brothers, I would go out with my cousins to steal little petty shit at flea markets and stores, then we would hit up a barbecue and meet up with more of our fam. Some nights, I didn't even come back home; I would spend the night at Link's house and get into some shit.

At one point, Rodney and I were hanging out a lot, and then he went to prison. He would always write me letters and encourage me to have a relationship with my mom. He would call me often and make sure that I was okay and talk shit about what we would do once he got home. Once he came home, I clung to him. We both have the same father, but he was more of a father to me than my actual father.

Naturally, like any little brother who looked up to his big brother, I wanted to be like Rodney. He was good looking, had money, and everybody loved him. I always wanted to be that. I always wanted what he had: the cars, flashy clothes, and jewelry. He was our backbone. He gave us a sense of security because people in the city feared him—nobody would fuck with us. One time, my older cousin punched me because of something petty, and Rodney was pissed. He was in prison at the time, but when he got out, he went to my cousin's house with a gun.

"Don't shoot me in front of my kids!" he cried. Rodney was seriously going to shoot his ass.

Then, another time, Rodney came up to my school to scare the shit out of one of my teachers. Don't get me wrong, I was an asshole in high school. It was a survival mechanism. This day, I was clowning with one of my classmates and Mr. Peterson had asked me to stop.

"I didn't do shit," I retorted.

"Jason, please don't use that language in here. You're being disruptive. Please be quiet."

"I ain't no little ass kid," I snapped back at him. "I don't know who the fuck you think you talking to."

"I'm talking to you!" Mr. Peterson exploded. "And if you're going to be disrespectful, you can get the fuck out of my classroom!"

I was shocked. At the same time, I was pissed. I walked over to Mr. Peterson and said, "Make me, nigga!" He stood up like he was really going to try me, but then he called security instead. They escorted me to the office, and I was talking shit to them, too.

Later in the office, the principal had asked what happened.

"The nigga swole up like he wanted to do something," I reported.

"Okay, well, Jason, we've been having a lot of problems with you the last couple of weeks. You need to call your mom to come pick you up."

I wasn't going to call her ass. Instead, I called Rodney. I told him what had happened in class—at least, my version—and he was on his way. When he showed up, he had Link and my dad with him. That was one of the few times that my dad had my back, but he was probably just fronting for Rodney. When they came into the office, Rodney had asked if he could speak to Mr. Peterson. The principal told him that now wasn't a good time, so we waited in the parking lot until after school was dismissed. We saw Mr. Peterson walking to his car, and everybody jumped out.

Rodney grabbed Mr. Peterson and said, "What's that shit you was talking to my brother?"

I laughed and watched Mr. Peterson's eyes grow bigger.

"You disrespect my little brother again, and I'mma fuck you up, yo."

I didn't have any problems with Mr. Peterson after that, but I didn't last that long in school anyway. I had gotten kicked out and was on my way to dropping out of high school completely.

***

During the early '90s, the Caprice Classic was the car that everybody in the hood wanted to have, including myself. Rodney was already rolling around in his own Caprice, so I went to Rodney and told him, "Yo, I want to be you. I want this lifestyle. I want it."

He told me straight up, "The only two ways you're gonna get it is by getting in these streets and selling dope, or you're gonna go to school."

The answer seemed easy enough because I already had a "fuck school" disposition. I struggled with school. I didn't want to be around people. Because I still struggled in my day to day interactions with the other kids, largely due to being so institutionalized, I got kicked out of public school and went to an alternative school. I didn't like the teachers there, so I left, went and got my GED, and went to work.

"I want to sell dope. Fuck it. I want to go the fast route."

I was already in the streets, so he gave me an eight ball and a gun. My boy, Spencer, and I went down to a bridge downtown that was dark, dangerous, and full of drugs and crackheads. I stayed there all night trying to sell the dope my brother gave me, and I didn't know what the fuck I was doing. I didn't know how the politics of dope dealing worked. I didn't know you don't negotiate with crack heads, and I was completely ignorant about not letting anybody else sell dope on your block. I wasn't a drug dealer. I was just trying to figure it out.

Just my luck, the police came and chased Spencer and me down the street. We hopped into a garbage can, and as we were hiding, I was trying my best not to have an asthma attack.

"Nigga, hold your breath!" Spencer whispered loudly, "They gone hear us!"

"This shit is too much!" I snapped back.

I had spent the night running, damn near losing a lung, and hiding in garbage cans— I was so young, and I had no business even at the bridge that night. To top it all off, I had lost some of the dope.

I called my brother at 6:00 in the morning, "Yo, can you come and get me?"

"Where you at?" Rodney cleared his throat.

I told him my location and he came to pick me up with a jerry curl bag on his head. I handed him all the money that I had—it was crumbled up and the bills were in no type of order. I was pulling money out of everywhere, and I was showing him the dope that I had left. It didn't add up.

Rodney looked at me like I was crazy as hell. "Where the fuck is all the work? What happened?"

I was fumbling around trying to explain to him, "Well this person didn't have it, so I'm gonna get it from him later. This person said—"

"You don't get money from a crack head later!" He breathed a heavy sigh and shook his head. He knew I didn't know what the fuck I was doing. "This ain't for you."

A couple of weeks later, Rodney went with me and enrolled me in college. He paid for all my books and drove me back and forth to school. I liked the classes that I took in college, but I didn't like college. What I appreciated most about my brother allowing me to sell drugs was that he helped me figure out that it wasn't for me. I had to have a different plan, and I quickly realized that as much as I admired my brother, I wasn't like him.

4

AN INTRODUCTION TO A QUEEN

A LTHOUGH I WAS ROLLING with my brothers most of the time after I left foster care, I didn't want to neglect my little sister, Tamica. We made plans to go to the San Joaquin County Fair; the fair was notorious for bringing major Hip Hop and R&B artists to the stage, and this year, Queen Latifah would be performing. My sister was a huge Queen Latifah fan, so she insisted that we didn't miss the fair that year. "Living Single" had just come on the air, and it was a big show. I was only about 15 years old, but I really appreciated her artistry and her influence in the entertainment industry. I was always infatuated with the music and entertainment industry because I loved to see Black people being amazing, talented, and successful. I wanted that. I wasn't a rapper like her, and I didn't know exactly what I wanted to do, I just knew I wanted to be in the industry.

My twelve-year-old sister and I went to the fair on our own. In the streets, again, two peas in a pod. We finally made it to the fair, and my sister had a mischievous grin on her face.

"You want to go backstage?"

"Let's go." I didn't hesitate.

I let her lead me all the way past the cows, pigs, and shit. We slipped right past a herd of cows and a bunch of saddles and rope on the left side of the stage. We made it to the back of the stage and saw a gate guarding the backstage entrance where Queen Latifah was. We saw that nobody was looking, so we climbed over the fence. We thought we were in the clear until we ran into a security guard who looked at us suspiciously.

"How did you guys get back here?" he grilled us.

"Oh, we had our passes because we're with the tour," I lied. "We're with the people, but somebody just stole our passes."

My sister was playing along brilliantly, and our lie was so good that the security guard went and found us some backstage passes. We played cool, but we were geeked as hell. Honestly, I don't know how we pulled that one off. We were *kids*. Nonetheless, we were hanging out backstage knowing full well that we had no business being back there.

As we perused the backstage area, I saw Queen Latifah come outside getting ready to leave. I rushed over to her to make sure I could at least meet her before she left.

I boldly placed myself in front of her and said, "Hey, how are you? We're fans. This is my sister, Tamica. I'm Jason."

She was cool. We started shooting the shit and going back and forth. Here was my chance. "Yo, you know, do you sign artists? My cousin Ruben is a rapper..."

"Well, where is he?" she replied.

"He's here in the fair." I was so shocked that she was even entertaining me while I was talking to her about an artist. I knew that I didn't have a talent that I could pitch right then, so Ruben was my saving grace.

"Well go find him," she demanded. I did everything I could to find his ass. He came backstage and rapped for her. He gave her his CD, and then we all stayed backstage still kicking it.

I was about to shift the conversation and kick some real shit to her, whatever that was, but as soon as I started to speak again, she turned away and started talking to some other people and signing autographs. *Damn, I was trying to get an autograph, too,* I kicked myself. I decided that I wasn't going to play myself. "Excuse me," I yelled out to her. "We've been waiting here the longest. Can we get the autograph?"

Queen Latifah chuckled and said, "What?"

From there we were going back and forth with each other jokingly talking shit like we'd known each other forever.

Then I made an even bolder move: "Give me your number," I demanded. "I want to stay in touch."

Her eyebrow must have raised three inches. "Give you my *number*? Boy, if you don't get out of here!" She laughed while getting inside of her van, but I stood my ground. "I'm not giving you my number," she said, hanging out the window. "If it's meant to be, you'll find me."

I resolved to track her down somehow. I really liked her. There was something about her that captivated me. She was cool and down to earth, but more importantly, she was someone who was where I wanted to be professionally. The fact that she acknowledged me made me really want to pursue the relationship.

***

Three days later, I was set to spend the night at my grandmother's house. I needed to make a few runs, so I called my brother, Link, to pick me up. He arrived around 9:30 am and let me know that he needed to get a car wash before we headed to our destination. He had a Caprice Classic, and amongst the guys in our crew there was an unspoken rule that you never drove around in a dirty car. Especially a Caprice. It was cool. I got in the car, and shortly thereafter, we were at the car wash. This establishment was where some of everybody hung out. There were crackheads, and all the homies there getting their cars washed, too. People were playing music—my brother's being the loudest, of course—and it just seemed like a real chill Saturday morning. I was sitting in the front passenger seat, and he was outside cleaning the car.

After some time, I got annoyed at how long it was taking him to finish washing his car. The sound system continued to roar and thunder, playing Janet Jackson's "Anytime, Any Place." It was so loud that I couldn't hear anything around me. Annoyed, I got out of the car and urged my brother to hurry up.

"Bro, you taking forever waxing your tires and shit."

He looked up at me with a smirk on his face, knelt back down, and continued to wipe some more. I walked up behind him and made my request clear: "Yo, we need to go."

Before I could even say much more, we heard a "boom." It was the loudest bang I had ever heard. It was leading up to The Fourth of July, so I thought somebody threw an M-80 bomb—one of those big, loud firecrackers.

"Who the fuck..." I trailed off before noticing that the thigh part of my pants had exploded. My pants were hanging and frayed, and I was pissed because I thought somebody threw an M-80 at *me*. My brother jumped up. He had been shot before, so he knew what was happening.

I saw the panic spread across Link's face, and I was confused. I didn't know what was going on, but everybody was hysterical. A couple of seconds passed, and a crackhead ran up to me yelling, "You shot me!"

Everything was hazy, and I had no idea what he was talking about. "I shot you?"

He was holding his hands together and blood was squirting out of them. Blood was everywhere.

My brother, sensing that it wasn't an accident, ran to the car and grabbed his gun. Then I heard another "boom," this one seeming a lot closer than the last. The grocery store window across the street from where we were shattered. Then I understood what was happening: we were getting shot at. I didn't know why, and I didn't know who the shooters were. All I knew was that we needed to get the fuck away from there. Janet was right: shit could pop off at "anytime" and at "any place" where we were from. That's not quite what I had in mind though.

Right after the glass shattered, a frantic lady ran up to me and shouted, "Baby, you got hit!"

"What are you talking about?" I challenged. Everything happened so fast that I didn't even feel the wound. I looked down, opened my pants, and there was a big ass hole in my thigh—maybe three or four inches in diameter. The bullet had cut right through. Whoever pulled the trigger didn't hit me directly; the bullet had gone through the man's hand, hit the wall, ricocheted, hit me, and then hit the other wall. The second bullet went across the street, through a girl's back, out her chest, and into a guy's side. The shot blew his chest out and killed him. The four of us had gotten shot with just two bullets. Later, I found out that I was shot with a 30

OT 6 rifle, also called an elephant rifle. The bullets were big and long—shit, to shoot an elephant I guess.

"Let's get in the car!" I yelled at Link. "Let's leave!"

We jump in the car and drove off.

Once we got in the car, I was able to do a closer examination of my bullet wound. I saw the meat hanging out and my blood boiling. The jeans were burned into the wound, and my pants were all blown out. I was in complete panic, and my anxiety kicked in.

"Oh shit! It hurts!" I screamed at my brother. "Them niggas blew my fucking leg off!"

"You good!" Link was trying his best to calm my nerves, but I had no idea if I would live or bleed out on the backseat. He was driving so fast that I was praying we didn't get pulled over and taken to jail while I had this big ass hole in my thigh. We finally got to Link's house, and I got out of the car. I just sat down in the driveway, and his wife came out, puzzled.

"What happened?"

"Call 911! Jason got shot," Link explained.

She stood there, blinked a few seconds, and repeated him, "Jason got shot?"

"Bitch, call 911!" he shouted back.

The ambulance picked me up, and my whole family was headed to the hospital.

***

Once I arrived at the hospital, they took care of me pretty quickly. I was a lot calmer after I was finally stitched up and in some new clothes. The wound didn't seem as bad as it did with boiling blood and all that. I was glad that I was going to be able to walk and that I wasn't going to die. My brother talked a little shit about how frantic I was in the backseat, but I knew how nervous he was before we got to the hospital. I wondered if he knew who those guys were and if he had any plans to retaliate. I wasn't on any revenge-seeking shit, but I knew my brother. I didn't want him to do something stupid.

I was there for a couple of hours before my dad walked in. I wasn't thrilled to see him, but I appreciated that he thought enough of me to at least make sure that I wasn't dead.

"I would have never thought you got shot," he started. "I would have been out $6-$7,000 if you would have got killed."

I stared into his eyes coldly. *That's all you could come up with? At this moment, that's all you could think of?* I don't know if that was just the way my father shielded his emotions or if he was truly being an asshole, but I didn't appreciate it. He wasn't there for me growing up, and he couldn't at least show a little bit of concern now that I was lying in a hospital bed? Damn.

Once everyone who came to visit me started to trickle out, I found myself just laying in the bed alone with my thoughts. I let myself drift back to three days ago when I met Queen Latifah. She said, "If it's meant to be, you'll find me." I had time to find her. I knew she was on "Living Single" and that the show was on FOX, so I dialed 411 in LA, and asked for FOX.

When I reached someone from the network, I said, "This is Queen Latifah's cousin. I was just shot. I'm in the hospital. I'm trying to find her. I can't reach my family."

"Oh my God!" the secretary gasped. "You need to call Warner Brothers Studios."

She gave me the number, and I called the studio. "This is Queen Latifah's cousin. I was just shot in a drive-by. I'm in the hospital."

They transferred me to Yvette Lee Bowser, the executive producer, and I told her the same story. "I can't reach my parents. I need to reach Dana." Yvette panicked and put me on the phone with a guy named Luther. I gave him the story as well. He transferred me to the stage manager, and then the stage manager ran the phone out to Dana's trailer. She had just stepped out, so I asked the stage manager to take my number. I went through all of that and felt like my luck ran out.

Well damn. I almost got there, I told myself. *She ain't gonna call back.*

But she called back. "Hello, Jason? What's going on?" I'm sure she thought I was somebody else, and she said, "Wait, who is this?"

I sat up a bit and tried to put a little "cool" in my voice, "This is Jason from Stockton."

"That little nigga with the mouth?" she shrieked.

"Yeah."

She sounded like she wanted to beat my ass, "You got everybody up in arms telling them that you got shot! Folks up here stressed out!"

I said, "No, I really did get shot."

She froze. "Why?"

I diverted the conversation, "That's not why I called. You told me if it was meant to be, I would find you. I found you, so what's up?"

She was amazed. "When you get out of the hospital, you and your friends can come to 'Living Single,' and I would love to see you."

I got out of the hospital that day. They stitched me up pretty well, but I still needed to stay off my leg for a while. Two weeks later, Dana gave me her Sky pager. I texted her, and she called me back. I told her that my friends and I were ready to come to the studio, and she let us come. We drove down to L.A., walked on set, and I never called her "Queen Latifah" again. We instantly connected. I walked around like, "Yo, I'm Dana's brother." I was really cocky. I made everybody know that Dana was my girl.

Dana and I connected so well that I was doing a little too much on the set of "Living Single." I was acting like a diva. I had this whole attitude that because I was Queen Latifah's friend, I was the shit. I walked around like, "Can't nobody tell me nothing."

After visiting the set a few times, Erika Alexander, who played Maxine Shaw on the show, had connected me with the talent department. They brought me in, and they let me be an extra on the show. Anybody else would have been humbled, but not me. My arrogance was just too over the top and I needed to be brought back to reality. I was waiting in line for food, and I decided that the kitchen staff was making me wait too long. I got loud and belligerent in the lunchroom, and I was being really disrespectful.

In the middle of my episode, Dana walked up to me real smooth and said, "Yo, let me holla at you." She pulled me outside and then told my ass about myself: "This is my fucking job. You need to relax and chill. Now you gotta come to my trailer to finish your dinner because you're doing too much."

She took me to her trailer, and I remember feeling like my consequence wasn't that bad. I got to hang in the trailer with Queen Latifah, so I saw it as a win.

My friends and I were going back and forth to the set of "Living Single" all the time. I truly valued the relationship I was building with Dana, not only because she was a genuine and caring person, but because she showed me a world different from the one I knew. The first time I came to LA, I saw Black people working—not killing each other, not selling drugs, but being productive. I fell in love with that world. It was enough for me to decide that I needed to be a part of it all. *Yo, I gotta get out here. I don't know how to get out here, but I gotta figure it out.*

5

LOVE ON THE LOW

W HILE I WAS MAKING BIG PLANS to prepare for my LA move, I realized that there were some things in my romantic life that I needed to figure out. "Love" was something that still eluded me, and I wasn't sure who or what that looked like for me. I was in a relationship with a girl named Nikki, and I thought I was in love with her. She was my girlfriend, but coming out of foster care and being in group homes, and not being around my family from age eight to 14, I really had a sketchy idea of what love was. I'd never been in a serious relationship when I was in those group homes, so this was my real, first relationship. I had girlfriends in the group home here and there, but in group home, you don't get to go out and see anybody. You saw them at school or you talked to them on the phone, but you didn't get to go to their house. You didn't get to go on dates, and you didn't get to hang out.

I was attracted to Nikki, but the more we were together, the more I wondered if I was in love with her because I really was or because it was expected of me. My brothers wanted me to have girl-friends and everybody in the city was always talking about how cute I was with my long, curly hair. People always thought that I was a ladies' man, but I was never like that. I never had a bunch of girl-friends. My brothers did, so I guess I was guilty by association.

The more I dated Nikki, the more I also discovered that she really wasn't a good person. She didn't reciprocate the love, atten-tion, and time that I was giving her. After a while, I was just going along with the motions, and just having a girlfriend for the sake of having one. We were sexually intimate, but that became the founda-tion of our relationship. Her dad didn't really like me—maybe be-cause I was banging his daughter out whenever he wasn't home. I guess I get it. Nikki and I were drifting apart and I was looking for more than what we had.

On top of that, I was facing an inward struggle; I had started to become attracted to guys. I had these feelings since I was about 14, but I didn't really act on them until I was 18. The first guy I had been intimate with was my homegirl's boyfriend. I know, scandalous, right? We were all hanging out one night, and I got a vibe from him that maybe he got down on the low. He used to collect CD's, and I used that as my opportunity to test my theory. I wanted those CD's because I love music, so I made my sexual encounter with him like a business transaction. I had to set it up that way so that it would seem okay to do it in my mind. If he wanted to mess around, I was all for it; I was feeling out his vibe so that I knew the right time to present my terms.

"If you wanna fuck, I'll do it, but I want these CD's."

He agreed, just like I had suspected, and we had sex. This was the first time that another male had touched me since my babysitter's boyfriend all those years ago. With each kiss, lick, and thrust, I wasn't sure if I was enjoying what was going on. When we were done, I got all the CD's, but I felt trashy—not necessarily because of the transaction, but it just felt wrong. I felt like I shouldn't have done that. I was still with Nikki when all this went down, so that made it even worse for me. It reminded me of the scene from *Set It Off* when Stonie had sex for that check. I was on some hoe shit. It also felt so wrong to have sex with another man.

I didn't do anything after a while, and I continued with my relationship with Nikki like nothing happened. Then I met another guy, and we messed around. We didn't have anything serious; he mostly served as an opportunity for me to explore if being with men was something that I actually liked. I enjoyed having sex with him, but I wasn't sure if it was just him I liked, the act itself, or both. I didn't have a way to "test" other sexual experiences with other partners because Stockton was not a city where people were openly gay. Truthfully, I didn't even know what gay was. I didn't know about gay clubs or Pride. I didn't know how to find other gay men, but this guy had mentioned that he had messed with a guy named Calvin. He worked at Taco Bell, which was down the street from my house.

I don't know what my end goal was, but I was thinking, *I'm going to ride through Taco Bell and see what this guy looks like.* I went inside and was met by two very effeminate guys. Then I noticed Calvin. He was masculine, good looking, tall, and brown-skinned.

Oh shit, I thought to myself. This was the first guy who I was attracted to that I really wanted to pursue, so I befriended Calvin. We exchanged numbers, and I would see him at parties around town. He didn't know that I knew about him liking guys, and I knew he didn't know about me. We became best friends, and we would hang out every single day. The craziest part of it all was that he lived across the street from my mom's house with his girlfriend.

Then we started to get really close. I was around 19 when I got an opportunity to appear on the "Ricki Lake Show." I called the show and came up with a bogus ass lie just so the producers would be convinced to let us on the show. Once I sold them my story, we were officially invited to be a part. The name of our show was called "Girlfriend, Lose Your Jealous Streak or Lose Me Today." I had two girls come with me; one was pretending to be my "jealous" girlfriend, and the other was pretending to be her best friend. I invited Calvin to play the role of my best friend, and he was thrilled to come along.

We got to New York and had plenty of time to kill. We had the show the very next morning, but we were just drinking and chilling. When it was time to go to bed, I turned the TV off and then there was this knowing tension. Calvin looked at me for a second, smirked and said, "Your ass is scary."

I knew what he was talking about. At least I hoped that we had been on the same page with all the time that we had been spending together. Calvin was giving me an invitation to be bold, and I took him up on it.

"I'm scary? The fuck I'm gonna be scary about? What are you talking about?"

He started flirting again, "You know what I'm talking about."

I played it cool. "You're the one that's scary."

The room was dark. We were both in separate beds looking at each other face on waiting for the other to make the first move. It wasn't that easy, even though I had been with other guys before. Our flirty banter continued.

"I know wassup," Calvin responded. "What's good?"

I had enough of all the coded talk and indirect invitations. "Well," I began, "closed mouths don't get fed."

He dismissed me, "Well I'm not trippin.'"

The moment was here. I decided to stop being afraid and go for what I had wanted all along. I got out of the bed, walked over to Calvin, and it was on.

The next morning, we did the show, and it was the most fun I'd had in a long time. I enjoyed everybody's antics and I could tell that the crowd was loving us and eating the shit up. Every now and then, Calvin and I would exchange glances during breaks, and I would feel a weird flutter each time we stole those moments. The rest of our time in New York was blissful—we explored the city side by side and had more intimate moments before it was time for us to return to our heterosexual reality.

From that point on, I was in love with him. That was it. I didn't want to be with my girl, and I didn't want to do anything else except be with Calvin. I fell in love with Calvin because he was a dope person, but also because he was the first person to really make me feel loved. It was already a budding friendship that was building up to an epic romance. We would sit in the car for hours writing, rapping, writing poetry, and exchanging poetry about life and things that we were passionate about. We had so many things in common; I thought we were very compatible.

When we got back from "The Ricki Lake Show," he enrolled in the college I was attending, and we would meet up and play dominoes. He would take me on trips with him to San Francisco, and that's when I learned why Calvin was always so fly—he was stealing clothes from San Francisco and selling them at a fraction of the price. He was a professional booster. I hadn't stolen anything of real significance since I was lifting jewelry off dead bodies, so Calvin taught me how he operated. We stole Tommy Hilfiger, Polo, Guess—you name it. We used to go and just steal shit all the time, and in a dysfunctional type of thrilling way, we became even closer. It was a Bonnie and Clyde type of relationship but on the retail level. Everybody in my family knew him, and I brought him around my brothers and my closest friends. I introduced him as my best friend even though there was obviously something more going on between us. I wasn't sure how to "come out" and let everyone know that I was in love with Calvin. That didn't fit who I was supposed to be or what I was supposed to do. I didn't know how to be openly gay, so no one could know about Calvin and me.

For a while, I enjoyed our secret romance. It was intoxicating to steal moments together and to have something that was so precious and special that the two of us were the only ones who could experience it. It was great being affirmed and free; it was great to have my heart love so relentlessly and passionately. But that wasn't what I wanted. I didn't want to feel like a side piece or option. I wanted Calvin to be mine. We were sneaking around so much, and I was completely over it. I was over my girl, and I decided to break up with her. The next time I saw Nikki, I let her know that we were done:

"Hey Nikki, I think we should end things."

"What? Why?" she scrunched her nose and gave me a side-eye.

"I just think we should go our separate ways. It's been kinda different between us for a while."

"So are you fucking somebody else or something?" she asked.

I lied and just told her that I wished her well. Breaking up with Nikki was a huge weight off my shoulders, and I couldn't wait to tell Calvin the news:

"You'll never guess what I did today!" I was trying so hard to keep cool, but Calvin noticed how hard I was trying not to grin.

"Whatever it is, you real geeked about it!" he smirked.

"I broke up with Nikki." Calvin's reaction wasn't exactly what I was looking for, and he kind of just left me hanging on my words without much enthusiasm on his end.

"Forreal," he took what felt like an hour to respond. "Why you do that?"

"The fuck you mean, 'Why I do that?' I want us to be serious with each other. I want to be with you, and I'm willing to do whatever it takes to get there."

"Forreal?" He kissed me and hugged me tight, but I could feel that something wasn't right. I didn't know how to address his lackluster response to me, so I just put it all out on the table.

"I love you, and you love me. Are you going to get rid of your girl, too?" I really thought he was going to break up with his girl, but he didn't.

"I don't think I can give you what you want."

"Why not?" I trembled.

"You want me to leave my girl, and I just can't do that."

"Why not?" I asked again more forcefully. I was fuming at this point. "We spend all our time together! We make love! We get each other, and you're my best friend. What the fuck does she even mean to you?" I was devastated because I really felt like we were at a point in our relationship where he would have left his girl for me. Our relationship was deeper than us just messing around, but he didn't feel the same way. He didn't want to leave her, but he was still cool with messing around.

I was crying. He was crying. We both knew it was over, but he begged me not to end it.

"You can't have your cake and eat it, too. We're not gonna do— I can't do this anymore. I can't mess around. I thought we were moving towards something serious. You don't want to commit."

I knew that was it, but I was still in love with him. It was harder than I thought to end everything cold turkey, so I struggled for the next few months trying to choose between my heart and my head.

6

RODNEY

———

H ERE I WAS THIS KID who had all the potential in the world and the opportunity to do what the hell I wanted in life. I had my world in my own hands, and I had been on my own since I was in single digits, and I had lived life how I saw fit. I had decided that the time was right to move to LA; in fact, I was moving the next morning. I decided to have a going-away party at the Eldorado Bowl, and I invited all my cousins, siblings, Calvin, and my friends. I had already told my mom and everybody else in my family that I was moving, so it was a special night. I appreciated how they showed up for me: everybody was there, including my brother, Rodney.

That night there were also some girls there—one of whom used to be my neighbor. Her name was Samima; I lived in apartment 70, and she lived in apartment 63. She was a Samoan girl with long, black hair, and she was there with her boyfriend, Phillip, who they called "Filthy Phil." He and I were friends. Samima got into an altercation with another girl who I knew from the southside; the argument got so heated that security took her outside. Rodney kind of shrugged off the spat, but at this point, I was done for the night.

The girls fought a little more, and Rodney was sitting at the bar. The funny thing is that Rodney was 6'5" and 230 pounds, but he didn't drink.

"Ah, nigga you know damn well ain't nothing in there but some water!" I hollered.

"Nah, it's a Sprite," he laughed.

People thought that Rodney was this tough guy because it looked like he was mean mugging all the time. The truth is that he couldn't see for shit, so he was always squinting and staring really hard. We laughed a little more, and then I was on my way.

"Alright, I'm about to go home, I announced.

"Okay, I'll talk to you later."

I told him, "I love you."

The thing about it that stood out the most was that I had never told him the words "I love you" before that night. Even in a letter when I was writing him in prison, I never said, "I love you." I told him that this night, and honestly, I'm glad I did.

He said, "I love you too," and then I walked away.

***

I was probably about 7-10 steps away when Samima came back into the club. I stood to the side a little bit because she looked like she wanted to fight. Phillip grabbed her from behind and picked her up, and she was screaming and fighting to get down, and then she pulled out a gun and started shooting.

It felt like everybody in the room fell on top of me, and then I saw her fall down right in front of me. Eldorado Bowl was a small venue, and there was only one way in and one way out. There was another door out, but it had chains around so it was useless as an exit. The only way to get out was to get past where she was standing—where she was with the gun.

Everybody who was in the club was ducking and scrambling to get out; I could hear the frantic screams and panic of the people around me. There was nowhere to run. There were people on top of me, and I was fighting like hell to get out of there. Eventually, Phillip dragged her out of the club, so Samima was gone. After the madness settled a bit, I ran out and stood outside waiting for Rodney to come out. It seemed like a thousand people came out that building, and none of them were him. He didn't come out. I didn't know what was going on, but I wasn't going to go back in.

I was still standing outside pissed that somebody spilled a drink on me when I heard more gunshots—this time they were outside. Samima was outside shooting at somebody else now.

"Bitch, I will fucking kill you!" Samima shrieked. She had put her hand in the car window and tried to shoot a girl in the van, but she missed.

Everybody was running back into the bowling alley with guns. There were guns coming in, shooting outside, and everybody was running around like fucking maniacs. I wasn't going to take my chances with Samima's crazy ass, so I ran back inside. I saw an easy enough escape route by way of an employee exit, and I ran down the side lane that led to the back of the alley. Once I got to the back, I kicked open the locked door, and I ran behind the bowling pins toward the emergency exit. I opened that door, got out of there, and found myself on the other side of a chain-link fence with circular barbed wire on the top.

Okay, shit! I was trapped. My next obstacle was making it over the barbed wire. Calvin's car was right over the fence, so I knew that if I got over, I'd be able to leave. I started climbing up the fence and was spotted by two ladies who were also running to their cars.

"Hey, ain't you Rodney's brother?" one of them shouted.

"Yeah," I replied, still not quite over the fence yet.

"I think he just got hit."

"What do you mean?" My heart started thumping hard and strong.

"I think he got shot, and it doesn't look good."

"What do you mean he got shot?" I was totally confused. I had just left him at the bar drinking his Sprite mocktail.

I leaped down off the fence, scratches and all, and ran back into the bowling alley from the front. Everything was in slow motion. All types of shit was going on around me, but I couldn't even process it because the adrenalin had kicked in so strong. I couldn't really hear everything happening around me, but I could see it. People running. The police showing up. I remember all of that. When I got to the bar, I saw a guy with two long braids standing over a body that was laying on the ground. There were other people standing around screaming and crying. Someone was giving him CPR. When I walked up close enough, my throat began to tighten, and I could feel myself get weaker. It was my brother, Rodney, but he had a hole right above his eye. There was blood everywhere. Even while they were giving him CPR, blood was coming out of his mouth and spilling down his cheeks. My brothers, Kris and Christopher, were standing there looking just as broken as me.

It felt like an out-of-body experience. I was watching everyone, including myself, over his body. It wasn't real to me. I wasn't crying, but my brothers were. Then the police, firemen, and paramedics came in. They took the lock off the exit door and put my brother on a stretcher. I'm sure they put him in an ambulance, but I was so far out of it, I barely remember him leaving that bowling alley.

Rodney's brain matter was on the ground, and people were step-ping in it.

"What the fuck?" I thought to myself, "I can't even believe this is happening."

***

My friends and I got into Calvin's car and raced to the hospital. We pulled up, and I sat in the car watching people coming to see about Rodney. I saw my aunt. Then my cousin came. My father walked in, and then my uncles, and cousins...

"Get out the car, y'all," I stoically requested. Everybody started piling out the car and I sat in the back seat and begged. "God, please don't ... God, please don't let this happen. This cannot be happening right now."

I sat in the car in complete silence hoping that this was all a nightmare. I finally found the courage to go in, and someone asked, "Did anybody call his baby mom?"

Rodney had just had a baby who was seven weeks old, and he lived with his child's mother.

I asked again, "Has anybody called her?"

I didn't think that anybody did, so I volunteered. "I'll call her."

I went over to the payphone and called her, not knowing what the hell I was going to say to her.

When she answered, I said, "Tanya."

"Yes?" she responded.

I took a deep breath and had a slight tremble in my voice, "Tanya..."

"Yes!"

I tried again. "I got to tell you something." She immediately broke down crying. Nobody had called her, but she just sensed in my voice that something was terribly wrong.

"I don't want to hear shit you gotta say!" she wept.

"You need to get to the hospital." The last thing I heard was her screaming and crying.

I hung up and went back to find Rodney. I ran into a nurse and asked, "Can you tell me what's going on with my brother?"

She looked over her glasses and responded, "Who's your brother?"

"Rodney Townsend."

"Oh, ok. He's in surgery."

It was a sigh of relief. I was thinking, *Oh well, shit, if he's in surgery then he's alive.* I still wasn't crying, but I was still in shock. Through my mixed emotions, I still felt a tinge of hope. Surgery. It was the thread of hope that I was holding onto with all my might. I kept telling myself that he was going to be okay.

Okay, he's in surgery. He's good. Why's everybody tripping?

I even got a little bold and went to everybody else like, "Why y'all crying? What y'all tripping for? He's going to be okay!"

A little bit later, I saw another nurse walking by, and I asked about Rodney's progress again.

"Hey, I've been waiting. What's going on with my brother?"

"Who's your brother?" she asked. By now this shit was getting frustrating as hell.

"Rodney Townsend!"

"Oh baby, he passed away."

She just said it matter-of-factly. No sympathy. She told me about my brother's death in passing. There was no build-up to it, she just said it. It was like she sliced my throat. I used to mock death scenes in movies—people falling on the ground, and they're like, "Oh my God," and they're crying and this and that. I was always like, "That's so dramatic," but it's so entertaining. This was no movie. I fell to the ground. I could not stand up. All I had the strength to do was cry.

***

Though Calvin and I broke up, we found it hard to let go of each other. He was trying to comfort me, but I couldn't even let him. He fought with me to let him hold me because I was inconsolable.

I eventually calmed down and started to walk toward the back where Rodney was. A police officer stopped me.

"You can't go back there."

My face was still fresh with tears. "I need to see my brother. There's just no way that he died. It's impossible."

The officer softened his gaze and said, "You don't want to see him like that. It's not pretty."

"No," I insisted, "I want to see him."

Calvin stood beside me and declared, "I'm going with you."

"No!" I starkly reproached.

"*No*," he insisted, "I'm going back there with you."

We headed toward the back to the room and the nurse stopped us abruptly. "Before we go in the room, let me explain to you what he looks like and what's going on. We did try to revive him. There's a hole above his eye, and his eyes are open. There's a tube in his mouth, and his hands are in plastic bags because we had to run a test for gunshot residue. There's also some discoloration. He doesn't have a shirt on, and there's blood everywhere."

I completely dismissed her. "Okay, open the door. I need to see my brother."

They opened the door, and I went in. I saw him. That was it. His death was finite, and there wasn't any more hoping or praying that I could do.

Why did this girl kill my brother? Apparently, the other girl who Samima was arguing with stole her jacket. They were friends at first, but when Samima saw her with the jacket, she got mad. She confronted the girl and then the argument escalated, and they fought. After the fight, Samima decided that she wanted to kill the girl, so she went outside and got the gun. She came back in the bowling alley with intentions of shooting the other girl, but instead, she missed and shot Rodney. My brother lost his life over a fucking jacket.

I got home at about 4 am. My mom leaped as soon as she saw me, and barked, "What the fuck are you coming in so late for? Who the fuck you think you are?"

I tuned out the rest of the cursing and yelling she was doing. I was 19, but I was still living at her house.

I was red and sniffling. "You know what? Not today. Tonight's not the night. You're not about to do that tonight," I snapped at her.

My mom looked at me incredulously. "What the fuck is wrong with you? Why are you crying?"

I hesitated, but I answered her anyway, "Because Rodney got killed tonight."

Her mood didn't change, and she didn't offer an ounce of sympathy. She folded her arms, shifted her hips, and said, "They should have killed *your* Black ass."

***

Rodney's funeral was one to remember; it was a true gangsta funeral. There were red rags everywhere—obviously in reverence of Rodney's gang affiliation. His casket was elaborate and decked out, and there were Hennessy bottles used as décor around the sanctuary. We were in a church, yet people were cussing and throwing up gang signs. My brother, Kris, was playing Tupac's "I Ain't Mad at You" and Richie Rich's "Do G's Get to Go to Heaven?" on the speaker. I was so pissed at him for that. We may have lived our lives a little crazy and had some fucked up ways of going about things, but I had respect for the house of God. It is a sacred place. I learned this while living with the Easters during foster care. I had invited all these church people, my former foster parents, the pastor, and first lady.

All my church family from back when I was in the foster home were there. I was so embarrassed because it was the most disrespectful thing in the world. I sat there listening to the songs until I couldn't take it any longer. I got up and had a woman who attended my church come up and sing a gospel song. I had asked my foster father to preside over the service, and I didn't want him to feel out of place. Pastor Easter prayed and preached, and it was a good way to send my brother home.

"It's ok to be sad," he began. "Everyone in here loved Rodney, and everyone will miss him."

I sank down in my seat. "But one thing we have to understand is that, if nothing else, God is in control. God is a comforter, and we will make it through this."

I looked down at my hands and saw them shaking violently.

"What can we learn from the senseless premature death of this young brother...father...son? We know for sure that we need to spread more love in this world. We need to stop being so quick to resolve our differences with violence and ignorance. We need to value life."

The rest of the funeral was hazy. I do remember random people telling me that they were sorry for my loss. I remember the wailing of my brother's baby mama. I remember the cloud of darkness that hovered over us. I don't remember all of Pastor Easter's words, but I do know that he did his best to eulogize my brother.

Pastor Easter died a week later. I couldn't understand how. He was just preaching and now he's dead? I internalized the grief of his loss and tried my best to be inspired to wake up the next day.

7

DEATH AND DESTRUCTION

I WASN'T THE SAME after Rodney died. I got heavy into alcohol and tried my best to stay extremely busy so that I didn't have to be alone with my grief. If ever I was alone too long, I'd think about Rodney, and when I thought about Rodney, I couldn't function. Flashes of his dead body haunted me. Sometimes I made myself sick to my stomach thinking about what he looked like. I wondered if I didn't have that party that night if he'd still be alive. I wanted to redo that night so many times, and the fact that I couldn't was too much for me.

I mourned Rodney mostly by myself. I didn't have a relationship with my mom where I could receive comfort from her. I couldn't mourn with my dad because I didn't have that relationship with him, either. Calvin was still a part of my life, but he didn't really know how to support me. Of course, he would check on me, but I was so angry and so ready to snap that people just gave me distance. They didn't get in my way. When Rodney died, my whole disposition in life was "fuck it."

I was grief-stricken and I was angry. It was like I flipped a switch and became a lot colder to people and a lot less trusting. I shut down and didn't allow people to get close to me anymore, so my relationships suffered a lot. There was one person who I opened up to about my brother—Dana. She had lost a brother, too, so she was able to relate to a lot of what I was feeling. She stayed on the phone with me, encouraged me, and she returned every call that I made to her to try to process what was happening to me. Dana was the person I leaned on. She let me come and visit her—she was accessible. I had eventually pushed people away with my shitty disposition, and for a while, I didn't care. There was more drinking and more wallowing in my loss. I would reminisce about something crazy Rodney would say or do and get pissed. There were people responsible for his death, and I needed a way to make them feel the pain that I felt.

***

I made a mental list of all the people my brother was at odds with, and I made it my promise to avenge him. The night before Rodney died, there were some girls who were trying to break up his relationship with his girlfriend, and they started to be a huge problem. I remembered that he told me about the situation, so I arranged for some rough girls from the south side to find the other girls and beat their asses. The day after Rodney died, I was having a nervous breakdown, so I decided to go to the club to try to regain some type of sanity. First, I headed to the mall, but I got bombarded with people who had heard about my brother, and I was trying my best not to snap.

I went to the club, and I was "The Walking Dead"—not much life inside of me, but still trying to function. I was a complete mess, but then I happened to run into the girls who my brother had mentioned a few days before. Fire erupted within me.

I walked up to them and I said, "I know what y'all did to my brother. Before you leave, I'm going to have some girls beat your ass. You're not going to leave here without getting your ass beat."

They tried to sneak out, but the south side girls were at the club, too. They caught the other girls and beat them up so bad, but I didn't even care.

Then, my brother, Kristopher, told me about some guys who had robbed Rodney during a dice game a while back, so we were getting ready to handle them, too. I called one of my military friends, his friend, and my brother-in-law, Norman. We all got guns, hoodies, and masks, and we went to one of the guy's houses. I had my friend park on the street.

"This where these niggas stay?" I asked Kris.

"Yea," he confirmed.

"I don't give a fuck who in there," I declared, "I'm blasting everybody."

I could feel darkness infiltrating every sense of morality I had. We walked up to the building, went all the way up the stairs, and walked down the hallway. We were so cold-blooded and enraged that if anybody would have walked out of their apartment that night and seen us all walking in the hallway, they probably would have died.

We knocked on the door. Kris had a bat, and the rest of us had guns. These were real guns, too—I had a 40 magnum, my brother-in-law had a 357, and then my other friend had another type of gun that wasn't that easy to obtain. I pointed my gun directly in front of the door, and I made up in my mind that I was going to shoot whoever opened it along with everybody else in the room.

We were on a rampage. The sadness of my brother's death was always coupled with anger. As bad as I wanted to take out all my emotions on Samima, the girl who killed Rodney, I knew that I couldn't. She was locked up. No one answered the door, so we left. I was pissed, but had somebody answered the door, everybody in that apartment probably would have died that night for sure. I'm actually grateful that our plan failed. I would have become a murderer, and my brother would still be dead. I would have been locked up for the rest of my life and thrown my entire future away.

***

Things were getting worse for me after Rodney's death, and I felt like Death was unrelenting. I felt like I was losing everyone around me. My friend, Jerry, got murdered a week after Rodney died. I was at a club with his cousin, who was my brother's best friend and one of the pallbearers at his funeral. I went across the street to get a burrito, and Jerry was standing outside. I was like, "Hey, what's up?"

"I'm chilling, man, what's good with you?" he replied. I went into the spot, got the burrito, and when I came out, he was lying on the ground bleeding from a gunshot wound to his head. The blood made a shallow pool on the curb.

The Eastside Boys killed him. When I came out, they were standing right there and were sliding along the wall trying to get away before the police arrived. I had to go back in the club across the street and tell my brother's best friend that his cousin had just been shot in his head outside. It was crazy.

***

Steve's death hit me hard as hell—partly because I felt responsible. I had a friend named Japora, who was married to a girl named Cynthia. Japora was in prison for a drug-related crime when she met Cyn. She sold dope and was a well-respected baller in our community; because we were so cool, she would let me borrow her car from time to time. One of the times Japora gave me her car, I called my friend Steven and said, "Yo, Steve, I'm about to come pick you up." He was down, and I was on my way.

On the way to pick Steve up, I got caught up and lost track of time, so I was a little late. I was heading to the southside to pick him up; the southside was an area where all the ganstas and dope boys used to hang out. I never had any problems there because they all knew my brothers. There had been a few conflicts with other people, but I'd never known anything too crazy to pop off there.

When I pulled up to where Steve said he would be, there was yellow tape surrounding one of the buildings. *Yo, what's happening?* I thought to myself. I didn't see Steve anywhere, so I went to his house to find him and get the scoop on what had gone down. He wasn't home. I went back up to the turf to find out who was killed, but I was so nervous because I knew it was probably Steve. Apparently, he was shooting dice with a guy in a wheelchair named Denzel, another person from the hood who had been shot and paralyzed. Denzel and Steve got into an argument; he thought Steve was trying to play him because he was in a wheelchair. As the argument escalated, Denzel rolled back and pulled a nine-millimeter out from under his chair and shot Steve nine times.

He killed him over $10. I felt guilty because I was late. I felt like if I had been there on time, he wouldn't have died.

***

Jovon was a kid who I will never forget. I was attending Delta College when Rodney was murdered, and I had met Jovon there. He was young and attractive—he was flashy with his clothes and jewelry and was a "flyboy" who sold drugs. We would see each other at parties and mixers around town; he was cool for the most part. We were about the same age and I had been around drug dealers all my life, so I recognized his vibe.

When Rodney died, I tried to go back to school and resume my life, but I was just crying. I was severely emotional because it was extremely overwhelming. During one of my breakdowns, Jovon and another guy walked up to me and he said, "Hey, bro. There ain't no time to cry. Life is what it is, and you got to toughen up. You got to just deal with this shit."

It was the most insensitive thing anyone had said to me. There were actual Bloods offering their condolences to me, so him saying that really pissed me off.

"You need to stop being soft," they continued. "These are the streets. You know what it is."

I looked at them like, *Are you fucking crazy?* I get it: most of us were very desensitized and we had no emotion because of the ruthlessness in our community. We were surrounded by so much violence and death that many of us became numb. But this one really hurt, and it didn't just hurt me.

A few months later, I got a call from my friend, Bernice. She was frantic and she told me something that I couldn't believe: Jovon had been murdered.

"*What?*" I yelled. I got more information from her and immediately went to the scene of the crime. There was yellow tape all around the apartment complex. Bernice told me that Jovan was at home when a guy knocked on his door asking to buy crack. Apparently, Jovan opened the door and the dude immediately stabbed him with a knife. Jovan tried to get away, and he was running down the hall, dripping blood, and calling for help. As he was running, the guy was still stabbing him and he cornered him in the bathroom. He had stabbed him 33 times and then hit him in the head with a hammer. After he killed him, he went back into Jovan's apartment and robbed him. There was blood all over the walls and all in the bathroom. It was so traumatic how he died, and I couldn't believe that happened to him.

A few weeks later, I saw Jovan's friend—the same friend who had told me to stop being soft and that this wasn't the time to cry. When I saw him at school, he was a wreck. I walked up to him and offered my condolences and said, "Now you get it. Now you feel what I feel."

***

I was losing friends left and right, either by someone else's hand or due to betrayal. Tanisha's death was one that affected me in multiple ways. She was a friend who I had known since middle school; we were in the same math class together. She used to always wear red beads in her hair. She was a sweet girl, and everybody liked her. I didn't have many friends in middle school, but she was one of the few people who would be nice to me even when everyone else liked to fuck with me.

Tanisha and I were attending a graduation party, but when we walked in, we noticed that there were all white people. They were looking at us like we didn't belong there. My friend, Sandra, was also there and she could also sense the uneasiness in the room. She casually pulled out a little black lighter to light her cigarette, only it was shaped like a gun. To a person who happened to glance in her direction, it looked like she had flashed a gun before she put it back into her purse. We could tell that they didn't want us there, and the event was becoming more and more tense. We decided to leave, and so we headed out.

As we started to leave, a guy named Roger showed up with a bunch of people. When Roger arrived, the white people from the party came outside with a gun and started shooting into the air. I was chatting with Tanisha, who was standing outside of my friend Aaron's car. As soon as she heard the gunshots, she took off running. More gunshots followed, Aaron hopped in the car, and we drove off. We didn't know what happened to her or anyone else, but a few hours after, the police came to my house accusing me of shooting Tanisha. Tanisha's family thought that I was involved with her death because I was the last person she was seen talking to. I was shocked that she was dead and that they thought I did it.

Tanisha was dating Rodney's best friend, Brandon, at the time. Brandon also questioned if I had something to do with Tanisha's death, and I told him that I didn't. I cooperated with police and told them what I saw that night, and then I found out that the police arrested Roger as a possible suspect. As a result, Roger's friends were on the hunt to find out who had snitched on him, and for some reason, Aaron had given them my name.

The night that Roger's friends confronted me about Tanisha, I was out with Kris, my roommate—a Panamanian dude whose name I forgot but was crazy as fuck, and my best friend, Tasha. We were sitting around chilling when I got a call from Aaron.

"Where are you at?" he asked.

"I'm at El Torritos watching the game," I responded. A little after we hung up, he pulled up with a few guys who were obviously Crips. My brothers were Bloods, so I was already uneasy about this whole situation.

"Yo, can you come outside?" Aaron asked. I didn't suspect anything crazy, so I came outside.

When I came out, the guys got out of the car and started to confront me: "Yo, cuz, we heard you snitched on my nigga!"

I didn't know what the fuck they were talking about. All I knew was that Tanisha was dead. I didn't know who did it or why. Roger's friends said that they heard I had said something about Roger and that Roger was in the car with us that night. I found out through the newspapers that Tanisha had run away from talking to me, gotten caught in the crossfire, and allegedly shot by Roger on accident. I didn't see any of that; my only knowledge of what happened was based on what I'd seen on the news.

"Nigga, *snitched?*" I defended myself. "First of all, why would I snitch? Y'all already know I'm a real nigga."

They were like, "Well this is what we heard, so what the fuck you gotta say about that?" They were really pressing me. There were three of them, and my friend Aaron was sitting in the car with a goofy ass look on his face. I was thinking, *Aaron you brought these niggas here to get me?* I felt like he betrayed me.

"Okay, tell me this," I retorted, "who told you I snitched? Because if they told you that, let's all get in the same room together and let's talk about it." One of them looked at Aaron, and that's all I needed. I had plans for his ass. *I'm gonna get this nigga when they leave. You brought them to me like this. You set me up.*

I was already looking at Aaron sideways, so I said, "Who snitched?" They looked at him, and so I looked at him. I said, "Nigga, you told them that I *snitched?*"

Aaron got out and ran to the other side of the car. I had a knife in my pocket, and I pulled it out and chased him around the car. I guess this was the time in Stockton for niggas to be getting chased with knives. I didn't know what I was going to do when I caught him, but I knew I was going to get his ass. He was running around, so finally I was on the opposite side of the car, and I started stabbing one of his tires. Then I scratched his car with the knife.

"No! Stop, stop!" Aaron screamed. "You're fucking up my car!" I didn't care.

My friend and my roommate came out to me, and they were both yelling, "Jason put the knife down! Jason put the knife down!"

Then I yelled to Aaron, "Nigga, I'm gonna put the knife down, but you got to stop and catch an ass-whoopin'."

He stopped where he was, and I threw the knife down. I ran around and I beat the shit out of him outside of El Torritos. I fucked him up: I had a knee in his face, his head was in the ground, and I was punching him. I broke my thumb, and I ended up going to the hospital. I told him that he needed to come to my house and get his ass whooped because he had fucked up my pants. Well really, I fucked up my pants because I beat him up, but I didn't care. I still called him:

"Aaron, come over here to my house because I'm gonna whoop your ass." I was serious. I was going to fuck him up again.

"What are you talking about?" he questioned me. "Why are you tripping?"

"Aaron, come to my house and get this ass whoopin' right now! You're gonna get it one way or another."

Aaron brushed me off. "You ain't the same no more. Ever since your brother died, you been on some real crazy shit, bro."

I wasn't trying to hear anything he had to say. About a half hour after I had gotten off the phone with Aaron, our friend, Chae, called me.

"Hey, Jason. Aaron called. He said you called him and you was gonna whoop his ass." Aaron's punk ass had the nerve to call and snitch on me...*again?*

"Yeah, I'm gonna whoop his ass," I confirmed. "It ain't none of your business, so don't worry about it." Chae was trying his best to reason with me and talk me out of it, but there was nothing he could say to change my mind.

Aaron eventually talked me out of whooping his ass, and he ended up buying me some new pants. We didn't get in a fight again, but I had stopped talking to him.

***

Chae and I remained close. One night we went out to a club in a small nearby town, Angelino's, and this guy got into an argument with Chae. I was like, "Yo, my man, I'm really not for all the yelling. All the arguing, and all of that, let's bring this to a conclusion. Meet us at the gas station down the street."

There was a Chevron on the corner, so the guy was like, "Yeah this is whatever. We gettin' there."

106

We all got into the car and headed to the gas station. Without missing a beat, I got out of the car with my brother's 40 Magnum. I popped the gun, pointed it at him, and was dead set on shooting his ass.

He looked at me and said, "Nah." My friend JP and his brother, Jay, were also there. JP shouted, "No, no put the gun down! No, don't do that!"

I didn't shoot him, but I was really with all the shit when my brother died. I didn't care. There was nothing that anybody could do to make me give a fuck about life, and every day I was led by my emotions and ready to be reckless.

8

FORGOTTEN

A FTER THE POLICE INVESTIGATION and after overwhelming support from the neighborhood and everybody who had witnessed the shooting, Samima was charged with 1st-degree murder. I had awaited the day that she would get what she deserved, and I couldn't wait to look her in the face while the judge put her away for the rest of her life. She was reckless and irrational that night, and because of her lack of judgment, my brother was gone. I honestly wanted to see the bitch fry.

On the morning of the first hearing, I felt heavy. There was an eerie feeling of darkness that threatened to overtake me even though I was hoping that there was going to be some type of closure to Rodney's death. I dressed the best I could for court—I didn't have too many suits laying around, so I managed with a button-up shirt and a pair of slacks. I hoped that the jury and the judge would take me seriously when it was my turn to testify. I hope that they would believe me when I said that Rodney had not attacked Samima and that she had acted in a way that placed everyone's life in danger.

My mind drifted back to that night and I thought of all the ways that Rodney could have still been here. What if I just stayed with him when all the shooting happened? What if I had just talked with him while he drank his Sprite? Shit, what if we had gone somewhere different altogether? I was overwhelmed again and felt like I needed to get myself together. I couldn't change the past, but I could impact the future. I was going to testify and recall every minute detail in order to put Samima away.

As I entered the courtroom, I saw what seemed to be everyone I had ever known. Community leaders, pastors, gangstas, niggas who fucked with Rodney—niggas who didn't. I didn't know if people were there to get justice for Rodney or if they were there to be nosy and get all the tea on the trial. Then I saw my brothers and my nerves calmed a little. We were going to get through this, and we had each other. My father was there, but I didn't really acknowledge him. He had been shitting on Rodney since he died, so I really didn't want to fuck with him. I sat in the area where I would be called up to testify, and in any other situation, I would have felt like a snitch. Had it been anyone else who was murdered, I probably would have been deemed one by the hood, but because of the clout and respect that Rodney had, we all wanted everyone who was responsible for his death to get their just due.

As a matter of fact, people were taking justice into their own hands. Rodney was so important to our community and so well-respected that people were really angry. People wanted to kill Samima and were attempting to put hits out on her in prison. I was really cool with Samima's boyfriend, Filthy Phil, who, by the way, was one of the first people I took down to "Living Single" to meet Queen Latifah. Because it was his gun that Samima used to kill Rodney, the whole community was trying to kill him, too. They were beating him—someone stomped his face until his eye popped out of the socket. He had a rough time after Rodney died just because of his association with Samima.

***

Samima entered the courtroom shackled and dejected. People started to yell and curse at her, but the judge was quick to restore order and begin the hearing. They read off a bunch of charges and legal disclaimers—it wasn't how I thought court was going to go. I thought it was going to be like TV when the prosecutor would get super emotional, point at the defendant, and accuse him or her of being guilty of every crime of which they had been charged. It was very humdrum: there were no outbursts and no inflated voices. It was straight to the point. I don't know what type of deal Samima's attorney arranged, but she pleaded guilty. That wasn't a surprise though: everybody had witnessed her kill Rodney. How could she say otherwise?

There were some other testimonies and other speeches given by people, but I was finding it hard to follow and I was becoming restless. I zoned out and found myself going back to happier times and better circumstances.

***

Aye, Jason, Rodney called out. *You a pretty ass nigga—long curly hair and shit. I know them hoes be after you!*

I would laugh and change the subject every time he would ask about my sex life. I wasn't ready for him to know that I liked boys, too. I knew that he would still love me, but I was still uncomfortable with who I was at the time.

If you need me to help you find some bitches, just let me know!

I didn't need his help, but it was funny that he would offer. Every time we went out, girls would go out of their way to let me know that they thought I was fine.

Just don't be out here getting these hoes pregnant and shit. You too smart for that.

***

"The prosecution now calls Jason Lee to the stand."

It was my turn to testify. I felt my heart jump into my stomach and my pulse began to increase. I didn't think I would be strong enough to go back to that night. I didn't want to fall apart on the witness stand in front of my entire community. I took a couple of breaths, stood up, and approached the stand. I felt like a million eyes were on me, and that made me so uneasy—but I was here to do a job. I wasn't going to let my brother down.

The prosecuting attorney walked over to me and asked me the same questions that we talked about during our briefing a few days prior.

"Did you see the defendant shooting a weapon on the night of Rodney's death?"

"Yes," I confirmed.

"What was everyone else doing when that was happening?"

"We were all running and trying to find a way out of the bowling alley. I had to escape out the back and hop the fence. Then someone told me that my brother got shot so I went back in."

They asked me more questions about the night of Rodney's murder, and I answered them in great detail. Then the prosecutors asked me something I wasn't prepared for.

"Is there anything that you want to say to the defendant about losing your brother?"

I froze and my jaw tightened. The whole time, I had been trying to keep it together and let the proceedings go on peacefully. But the lump I maintained in my throat was strong and I couldn't hold back any longer.

I looked Samima in the eye and said, "When you killed Rodney, you killed me, too. I have had nothing but anger towards you since he died. You took my brother—the one who loved me, protected me, provided for me...you took my niece's daddy away from her." I felt my face begin to flush, but I continued. "I don't know what beef you had that night with whoever, and it doesn't even

113

matter now. You made a decision that forever changed my life, and no amount of time you get today will fix what you did. I wish you would have killed me, too. That's the only way that I could get past what happened."

She didn't look at me.

After all the proceedings, witnesses and testifying, Samima was sentenced to 22 years in prison. At the time, I felt that the criminal justice system did Rodney a disservice. I thought that she deserved to spend her entire life locked up. When she got out, I was truly conflicted. I spoke to the DA to explore whether I wanted to go through a program where I would get to meet her and speak to her again. I told them that I would only meet with her if my niece would, too. I do think this is important because I need to be able to get to a place where I can close that chapter. It would give me the closure that I had been seeking for so long, but then what if it doesn't? What if I met with her and it re-opened every wound? I can't forgive her. More than me, I think it's important that Samima explains her actions to my niece. She should see how she left a young woman to grow up without a father. She needs to own that, and she needs to hear whatever my niece has to say to her.

***

I didn't leave for LA like I had dreamed. When my brother died, and after all the subsequent deaths, I stayed home and got a job at the group home where I had graduated from just a few years back. I was in a deep state of depression, but somehow I was on my old counselor's, Ed Fleming, mind.

"Hey, how you doing, pretty boy?"

I chuckled, "Chillin.' Doin' me."

"Ok, I see. I ain't mad at that. Listen, I heard about your brother...I just want to give my condolences to you."

"I appreciate that, Ed," I mustered up a little gratitude, but my response was still dry as hell.

"How you holding up these days?"

"I been doing pretty good," I lied.

"Well, that's good to hear. I want to meet with you and talk to you about being a counselor back at the ranch."

I was reluctant about the whole "counselor thing," but I met with him anyway.

"I think you'd be a good counselor because you've been through what these kids have been through," he elaborated. "You know this program. You know how it is to be in it, and you know how it is to come out of it. I think you could be a good role model and example."

I never thought of myself as the role model type, but somehow, hearing it from Ed made me think that maybe he was right.

Edwin Fleming had spent a large part of his life dedicated to helping at-risk youth. He was one of the few who was really passionate about his work and really had a heart for kids. I admired him a lot because he looked a lot like me: curly hair, light skin...fly. He looked like he could have been my father. He had a ruby and diamond Playboy Bunny earring, and he always drove a nice car. He used to always tout me around as his son, and I secretly enjoyed it so much. I continued to be rejected by my own father, so having Ed claim me meant everything.

I ended up getting the job. The ranch where I worked was owned by Edwin and his family, and it housed about 18 boys. I was only like 20, and those kids were fucking 14 to 18—not much younger than me. Prior to this job, I had worked at my old high school, so I was pretty used to having to be the "adult" even though I was surrounded by kids not too far from my own age.

Wilma, Ed's mother, was an evil woman. She smoked cigarettes with her dogs and had a little raspy voice. And then Pat, her sister, was a little overweight. They were the quintessential black woman: they were tough, they had strong personalities, and they were revered.

After Ed gave me the job, he said, "I want to get a picture of you." He went and got a camera, and he started taking pictures of me—which was kind of weird. I didn't understand why Ed wanted pictures of me. He was taking pictures *of* me and *with* me.

"You grew up to be a really amazing young man," Ed admitted. "I'm so proud of you."

I really did love Edwin. In spite of all the fucked up shit I had done in my life, Edwin was proud? He knew me when I was a motherless child angry at the system and angry at myself for who I was. On this journey of mine, I've made some horrible decisions and had been reckless, but Edwin saw...me. He looked past what I had done and saw me for who I was and what I could become. He took a chance on me, and I needed him to do that for me.

One night, I needed to talk to Edwin about something, so I called him. He had given me his personal number, and he never had a problem with me kicking it with him when I needed to. The first call just rang and rang until it went to voicemail, and that was odd for him. I called again, and he didn't answer, so I kept calling and calling. He still wasn't responding to any of my calls. I was really attached to Edwin, so I immediately started to get nervous. I was trying to figure out what was going on and why he wasn't calling me back, or why he didn't come down to see me. After my tenth or so call, his mother picked up the phone. Wilma was matter-of-fact. Not cold-hearted, but she wasn't an emotional person at all. She was really dry.

"Wilma, why is Edwin not calling me back? I've been trying to meet with him. I need to talk to him about something."

Wilma responded blankly, "Honey, Edwin is sick. He's just sick and he can't come to see you right now. You need to be patient with him, and he'll get around to it."

"What do you mean he's sick? I've been trying to get in touch with him all this time," I complained.

"Baby, Edwin has AIDS."

It was the most shocking thing I had heard. This took me all the way back to my brother again. I knew that this meant Edwin was going to die. After I spoke to Wilma, I quit my job and never came back. I never called Edwin back. When he died, some people from the ranch called me, but I didn't go to his funeral. I couldn't do it again. It was something that I regretted because he was someone who really cared about me. He was a role model, and he gave me something to look up to. I owed him the respect of honoring his life.

All these important people in my life were just dying left and right, so I developed a real fear of death. I felt that God must have forgotten about me because he allowed me to love and lose the few people who loved me back. I had to admit to myself that I was angry with God. He let drugs take my mother from me. He never gave me my dad. He took my brother for no reason. Randomly, some girl who had a problem with another girl shoots him accidentally. My best friend, Filthy Phil, was the boyfriend of the girl who shot my brother, so I couldn't be his friend anymore. My friends were dying, and God took my pastor—my foster father. Now Edwin, my mentor.

There's no way the God that I was taught in church is the same God that allowed me to go through all this bullshit. I stopped going to church and I didn't pray anymore. I didn't see the point.

***

I reverted back to how I dealt with tragedy best: callousness and anger. "I don't give a fuck" remained my personal mantra, and I was known for it. Calvin never really went away, and we always had a special connection. This time when I saw Calvin, nothing was the same, and our relationship was strained.

One night, we were driving in the car, and out of the blue, Calvin said, "Yo, I got some good news."

"Well, what news is that?" I was open to hearing some good news, but I was really suspicious.

He smiled and said, "I'm expecting a baby with Jasmine, and I want you to be the godfather."

I looked at him coldly, and I exploded. "Nigga, fuck your baby! How could you disrespect me and ask me to be your baby's godfather? You know what I just went through with my brother! You know how much I love you!"

My mouth continued to say more foul things, but my heart was saying, "I really don't want to love anything else. I didn't want to get too close to anything else that would make me feel the internal anguish and misery that I carry with me daily." I felt like I could lose anyone at any point. My heart couldn't take it.

In the past, Calvin would never argue with me. I would be extra, selfish, or full of myself, but he always fell back. Sometimes I would be sharp with him or say something smart, but Calvin was always cool and never allowed me to take him off his square. He would check me in a nice way, but never would really stand up for himself. While we were riding down Hammer Lane that night, Calvin slammed on the breaks. He started crying, but he was cussing me the fuck out. I can't remember everything he said, but he was so hurt by what I said because he wanted his best friend to share the love he had for his child. In my mind, that child represented a lifelong connection to the woman who was preventing him from being mine.

There was no way I could. I just couldn't do it. I shattered him. That really cemented the fact that we were never going to be the same again.

Calvin calmed down and brought his voice to a faint whisper. "You know, you said a lot of things in the past. You said *a lot* of ill shit. You've done a lot of hurtful things. I've let you talk crazy to me. I get that you are going through things, but how the fuck could you disrespect me like that?"

He really was coming from the heart. His desire for me to be his daughter's godfather came from a place of genuine love, but I was numb. He poured out all his feelings and every ounce of admiration and love he had for me. I was still statuesque. He started crying and screaming at me again, and my response to him pierced his gut.

"Nigga, I don't give a fuck. Drop me off."

9

AN ICONIC CONNECTION

IT HAD BEEN YEARS SINCE I'd spoken to my mother, and to be honest, I was thriving without her constant negativity and toxic behavior. I had gained other meaningful relationships, and I struggled with the fact that my mother would not be among the people who I truly cherished. I often wondered what it would have felt like if my mother tried a little harder to be a good mother. Where would I be? What would it feel like to be like one of those kids who get drafted into the NBA and NFL and be brought to tears with gratefulness because of the impact their mothers had on their lives? If I could have done all the great things I've done without her, how much more could I have become with her in my corner and depositing love into my life? Or maybe I wouldn't have developed what I needed to be a hardworking go-getter, and I'm only who I am today because I was forced to thrive on my own.

Later in my life, my mother did show that she was proud of me. When I became friends with Queen Latifah, and when I started to get on TV, I would get on the bus, and everybody knew who I was because she had talked about me to everyone. She would always pull out pictures of me and show people. I didn't know how to feel about this at first because her pride in me was a foreign experience. I didn't know if she was showing me off so that people would think she was responsible for my success or if she was just proud of *me*. I suspected that she was using what I'd become to validate her as a mother in the eyes of those around her.

There were different breakthroughs in our relationship. When she started to get really sick, she lived in a convalescent home; I would visit her there. It wasn't all bad. One time, after I left, I sent her some flowers and a card that said, "These are long overdue." That was my way of showing some sort of tenderness and appreciation to her. I remembered what Mrs. Easter told me about always honoring her. I still could never say the words "I love you" to her. It was the hardest thing. I couldn't do anything else because I hated her so much.

About a week later, I got a call from one of my cousins that my mother was in the hospital and that her condition had gotten worse. My cousin was the nurse manager at the hospital and she emphasized that I needed to come and see her. When I got there, my brother and sister, Paul and Tamica, were there, and they told me that she was dying. We were all in the ICU making awkward conversation, and my mother looked like she could have taken her last breath at any moment. She was crying and struggling to cling to life, but she mustered up enough energy to speak.

"I just want you guys to forgive me because I did the best that I could."

Immediately, I thought about when I was a 10-year-old kid in foster care begging for my mother to bring me home. It dawned on me that when she said she was doing the best she could, her best had nothing to do with me. She was admitting her own inabilities. She was telling me what she was unable to do based on her addiction. It took a long time for me to understand that, and I forgave her. She passed away the next day. I didn't have a feeling. I had previously established a rule that I don't mourn anything for more than three weeks—Rodney being the exception. I was at peace with her passing, and I was happy that she wasn't in pain anymore. She was chased by her own demons: she was raped by her father, she gave up her kids, she was a drug addict, and she felt worthless. It always came out in her behavior. Not to mention she was bi-polar and had issues with her liver due to drug usage.

In a sad way, I can say I don't miss her. Not to be calloused, I just don't have any regret for anything, and I don't wish things were different. I just resolved to move on.

***

In my time in L.A., I had developed many instrumental relationships over the years. I was still in contact with Dana (Queen

Latifah) and I valued how she gave me a taste of the entertainment industry by allowing me to shadow her on the set of "Living Single." It was great being exposed to all the behind-the-scenes work, and I knew that I wanted to work in that industry somehow. I also wanted to be an entrepreneur, so I spent some time trying to feel out how I could couple my love for Hollywood with my entrepreneurial desire. I didn't know what area of the business I wanted to get into, so when I first got to LA, I started hanging out on the scene. I became friends with Rob Kardashian, Chris Brown, and Rasaul Butler. We would party all the time, and I would be the plug—the guy who knew how to get access to certain things and certain people. People were big on being relevant in certain social circles and being relevant enough to get a little Paparazzi attention, so people would pay me just to host their parties.

A couple of weeks after my mother died, I was back home for her funeral when I had received a call from Kelly Price, who was also on three-way with Faith Evans. Kelly asked me if I'd be willing to help her put together a party to celebrate her Grammy nominations. I have always been a fan of Kelly Price, and Faith Evans was my favorite R&B singer, but initially, I was a little reluctant. I thought that Kelly was a little dated for what I was trying to do with my time, although she was talented.

I wasn't sure about the idea, but I said, "If we did a 'Heartbreak Hotel' reunion with Whitney Houston, I think it could be iconic." The ladies hadn't been together since they did the song. I reached out to Raffles van Exel, who was close to Whitney, Michael Jackson, and Prince, and I asked him if he could put me in touch with

Whitney Houston to see if she would come to the event. He called her and Whitney said that she would come. I was geeked.

A week before the event, my friend, "Freckles," called and said, "Hey, I need you to come meet me somewhere."

"What's up?" I inquired.

She just insisted that I meet her where she specified. I didn't ask any more questions, I just went to meet her. When I arrived, Freckles said, "Take a walk with me real quick."

I started walking with her; by that time I was a little antsy about where she was taking me.

"Where the hell are we going?" I asked again. She led me to a club called "Playhouse." When we got there, Ray J pulled up in a fancy car, and I just looked at her like, *You fucking brought me out to the club for Ray J? Really? I don't understand where the surprise is.*

This was in 2012, way before "Love & Hip-Hop," so I didn't have any ties or connections to Ray J.

Freckles said, "Come with me inside the club."

Curiously, I followed her inside the club, and we walked over to the VIP area. Whitney Houston was sitting there. I tried to hold my composure but I was thinking, *Oh shit, it's Whitney!* I had no idea what to do. I was just so excited, and I was trying to think of a way to introduce myself. *Wow, what do I say? Do I go up to Whitney?*

Whitney's goddaughter recognized me, and said, "Hey, I know who you are. I'm Amber, Whitney's goddaughter."

"Okay, nice to meet you!" I replied.

"I want to introduce you to my godmother."

I smiled and said, "Okay."

She walked me over to Whitney, and then Whitney looked me over. She said, "So you're doing this party?"

"Yeah," I confirmed.

She crossed her legs, leaned toward me and said, "Tell me who all is coming."

I gave her a list of everyone who had confirmed, "Ledisi, Kelly Price, Faith Evans, Keke Wyatt, Anthony Hamilton—"

"Damn, that's a lot of fucking power in one room!" Whitney interjected.

"Yeah, and we'd be honored if you'd come." I took the opportunity to reel her in.

"I'm definitely going to come," she told me. I lit up.

"Cool."

The day of the event, Whitney called me directly to confirm her attendance but to also ask me more specifics about the event and the performers. I was a little nervous because I didn't want her to change her mind if I told her something she didn't like.

"I don't want to walk the red carpet," she continued, "and I don't want to perform. I just want to slip in and be there to support."

I said, "Okay, yeah. No problem, no pressure."

I was disappointed. Of course, we really wanted her to perform, and we wanted her to be there on the red carpet on stage. I had been working with the Kardashians for a while, and that project was a flop, so I was hoping that this event would have been my "big break." To have a legend grace the stage for just a moment would have been golden. And to sing? It would have been as iconic as I had hoped.

That night, a person from Whitney's entourage called me and said, "Okay, Whitney's a few blocks away."

"Okay, great," I answered. I had met up with Pat Houston, Whitney's sister-in-law and manager, and told her how excited I was that Whitney was coming and how much of a fan I was. Pat and I clicked instantly.

When Whitney pulled up, the whole red carpet, all the photographers, and everybody else ran over to her car to try and take pictures of her. She rolled the window down and said, "Hold up! I want to make sure that I look good. Can you please get these cameras away from the car?"

"Absolutely," I responded. She looked beautiful, but I followed her directive. I turned to the photographers and said, "If you're not on the red carpet, we're going to pull your credentials, and we're going to ask you to leave." They tucked those cameras away and they all ran back to the carpet.

Whitney looked at me, smiled, and said, "Yo, I fuck with him. I like him!"

I said, "Yeah, me and Pat—we bonded while you were on your way. We're all family now."

"Oh okay. We're family?" she laughed. "Okay! Well since you were able to get everybody in check, I'm going to walk your carpet."

"Okay, cool," I blushed. I'm sure she saw how glad I was, and at that point, there was no sense in trying to play it cool. Whitney Houston was about to walk *my* red carpet. She fixed her hair and got out of the car. Then she and Bobbi Kristina walked the red carpet and talked to everybody; they were really nice. Shortly after, we escorted them to their section. Whitney wanted a bottle of champagne, so I had someone run to the store to get the exact brand she wanted, Dom Perignon. Later that evening, she went upstairs, and we put her on the side of the stage. Somewhere during the middle of the evening, Kelly Price started talking about her. Whitney walked up on stage with Kelly, and then she sang "Jesus Loves Me." I was floored. She told me that she didn't want to walk the red carpet and that she didn't want to sing, and she had done *both*. Everyone was eating it up. There was a minor altercation between her and another person, but I didn't see it. The night was amazing, and I was basking in all the work that I had done. I was looking forward to building a relationship with Whitney and my mind was cloudy with ways that we could connect again.

The next day, I was on a high because I felt like I had a successful event. I convinced Whitney Houston to come out, and everybody was talking about it. It was a live music event. Later Don Benjamin and I went to the Roc Nation brunch, but we weren't on the list. I told them that I worked for Vibe Magazine and that Don Benjamin was an artist for Interscope Records. Then we created a Gmail account for somebody who worked at Roc Nation, and we used that fake email address to create a fake confirmation. By this time, I was a professional at sneaking in places I didn't belong. I had a new set of skills since trying to see Queen Latifah backstage at the local fair all those years ago. I wouldn't have gone through all the trouble just to attend a brunch, but our whole reason for sneaking in was so that we could see Rihanna. After we met Rihanna, we left and headed to the Adidas Gifting Lounge, and I got a call from my barber.

"Hey, where are you at?" he asked as soon as I answered.

I said, "I'm in the car.

He paused and then continued, "You're not going to believe what happened. Whitney Houston just died. It's not on the news yet, but I just got a call from somebody's who's at the hotel. She's dead."

"There's no fucking way," I snapped. She died getting ready for Clive Davis's party that night. I had just seen her at my party the night before.

"No, she's dead, bro," my barber reiterated. "It's getting ready to break. She's dead."

We went into crisis management mode and it became a media frenzy.

I was still working with the Kardashians, and the only person I could think to call was Kris Jenner.

"Kris, I've never been in the middle of anything like this. It's just very overwhelming. I'm getting calls from every media outlet, and everybody's trying to find out what happened. The narrative that's out there is not true."

Kris put me on a three-way call with the president of E!, Suzanne Kolb. Suzanne and I went down to meet with the vice president of E! News to discuss the night of my event. I was able to give them the correct narrative for them to put in their specials and breaking news stories about Whitney's death. Kris Jenner was instrumental in helping me do that, and if it wasn't for her, I don't know how I would have been able to navigate through that tragedy.

When she passed away, there was such a firestorm in the media about whether she was on drugs, whether she died of a drug overdose, her last 24 hours, and a bunch of other questions. There were so many speculations about her life and about what she and Bobbi Kristina were doing. I had to file a cease and desist order on Kelly Price from talking about the event and talking about Whitney. I also sent a cease and desist out to all the people who worked for me that night. I went to the club and made sure they deleted all the tapes and any footage they had of Whitney. I did my best to protect that last 24 hours.

My team filmed everything, and we still haven't released the footage of that event. A year later, we did an event to honor her and Queen Latifah—everybody came out. Jordin Sparks, who was in *Sparkle* with Whitney Houston, hosted and performed at the event. We had performances from Lil' Mo, Kim Burrell, and a lot of other artists who also wanted to honor her. Even after that event, we never released that footage. We did a really good job of protecting her image and defending her against all the rumors, so in a way, I feel honored that I was able to spend that last day with her.

What's crazy is the fact that I was impacted by the deaths of two women within the same time period: my mom and Whitney Houston. Whitney's death had caused me more grief and unease than my mother's. I had met Whitney just weeks before her last day on earth, and I had done more to honor and protect her than I had done for my mother throughout my entire life. That's when I really knew that the negative impact of my mother's parenting would follow me well beyond her death. Despite everything that she had done, or not done, my mother taught me the power of forgiveness. I learned that just because I forgave her, it doesn't mean that what she did was okay. It also doesn't mean that I should pretend that she didn't hurt me or that my feelings weren't valid. It means that I won't let what she did continue to negatively influence me. I learned that forgiving people has nothing to do with them, but everything to do with me. I chose to no longer be paralyzed by unforgiveness.

10

SOBRIETY AND FATHERHOOD

THOUGH I HAD IMMERSED MYSELF in other projects and events, I
still hadn't learned how to properly process and deal with Rodney's
death. There was a duality to my grieving process. Externally, I figured out how to be productive and be all that my brother believed I
could be—things that would make him proud. Internally, I was destructive, gaining weight, drinking heavily, not having a proper
diet—not taking care of myself. My mental health took a huge
backseat. The first 10 years after my brother died, I consumed myself
with two full-time jobs and partying a lot. I woke up, I went to work,
I went to my second job, I came home, I partied, I passed out. I was
also promiscuous. Alcohol was numbing all the pain and sex was
making me feel good. It was all very toxic.

I did that for 10 years. I had to press that depressive shit down.

I didn't understand how much damage I was doing to myself. I would get drunk and become "the life of the party," but I was really a reckless drunk that acted out and did things that the sober Jason wouldn't do. I became an alcoholic. For years, I drank excessively, and I hated what I was becoming. I started to wonder if addiction was just a part of who I was because my mother had struggled with the same thing. *Of course not.* I wasn't a crackhead. Anybody who knows me knows I would never do what I perceived as reckless drugs: heroin, cocaine, crack ... meth. I would never do those things. I've done molly and ecstasy once or twice. I didn't see alcohol the same way I saw my mother's drugs, even though I used alcohol for the same reason—escapism.

Then I finally realized that I couldn't go on living this way. I came to that conclusion while I was watching "Oprah" when Dr. Phil was still a part of the show. There was a lady whose daughter had been killed, and she said she wanted to go on the Oprah show to tell her daughter's story. My heart bled for her as she recalled her experience coping with waking up every morning and not being able to hold her daughter or hear her laughter. Then Oprah asked her a question that really challenged me—she presented a crossroad to both myself and that woman.

"What's next?" That was extremely hard to answer for myself. What really was next for me?

The woman responded, "Well, my plan was to come here and tell my daughter's story, and then go back home and kill myself."

That struck a chord. I recalled my own depression and suicidal thoughts. I remember the days when all I did was cry because I didn't know what was next for me or how I could get past what had happened.

Dr. Phil then asked, "Why are you choosing to remember the one day she died instead of celebrating the 18 years she lived?" That stung me. I had forgotten all the memories with Rodney and had replaced them with the grief of his death. I focused on the fallout of my family and the isolation I felt in grieving by myself. We didn't even grieve as a family at all, so I didn't know who to turn to reminisce about the good times and keep the memories of my brother's life present. That show was what I needed to continue with my life. I was able to start focusing more on the memories of Rodney that were positive, and I was grieving less. I still get emotional thinking about Rodney, but I don't live it every day. It's a gradual process.

***

The next step in my healing process was sobriety. I was devastated at how Whitney died, and the fact that she was gone that quickly after I had just seen her was sobering. I wasn't really public with my decision to be sober, but before my 90-day mark, I was invited to the National Alcohol Beverage Control Association (NABCA) Annual Conference. It was a meeting of all of the alcohol brands in the world.

I remember flying out to the conference and thinking, *I've been sober for 90 days, and I'm really proud of myself. This is going to be a big test for me.*

I attended the conference in Las Vegas, and all was well. Then I got a call from my friend who told me that Grey Goose was having a party and to meet him at the hotel. I was at a crossroads. I had already been invited to one alcohol-centric event; attending another one would be pushing it. I threw caution to the wind and said, "Okay, I'm on my way."

When I got to the party, I was sweating like a sinner in church. The party was lit: I saw so many familiar faces and the excitement of it all really made me want to soak up the moment. There were drinks in abundance, but I still had some conviction about my commitment to sobriety. I turned down the first few drinks I was offered, but then I met the owners Grey Goose—they asked me to have a drink with them. I wanted to tell them that I had been sober for the past 90 days, but that would have sounded dumb as hell. Why would I be at a party thrown by Grey Goose, an alcoholic beverage company, if I was trying to avoid drinking? It was the same as being off crack for 90 days but chilling in a crack house. I was honored to be invited to drink with the Grey Goose ballers, and I felt that it would have been rude to turn down their invitation.

Well, if I have one drink, nobody will know, I convinced myself. I promised myself that I wouldn't get drunk, and I had two drinks. Right after I finished the second drink, Dana text me and said, "I just want to let you know, you're my hero."

I said, "What do you mean?"

She elaborated, "The fact that you've been able to go sober, and I'm dealing with my own sobriety, I really respect you." I was devastated. I was thinking, *Damn, she admires me for being sober and she doesn't even know what I'm doing. I'm fucking up over here.*

Dana was so supportive of my journey to sobriety that she even offered to go to an AA meeting with me. She wanted to go for both of us. I never took her up on that because my mother, who was a drug addict and an alcoholic, also went to AA. It didn't change her one bit. Also, I wasn't comfortable sitting around a room with a bunch of strangers talking about my inward struggles and how I used alcohol to cope. That wasn't me. After those two drinks, I had gone two years without drinking alcohol, and I felt so accomplished. Alcohol was no longer my "drug of choice," and I had figured out how to enjoy it without abusing it.

***

Before she died, my mother and I still had a bruised and battered relationship, so I didn't talk to her much. My visits to the convalescent home were the most we'd spoken in years because I didn't deal with her. When I was about 17 years old, she had given birth to another son. For eight years, I didn't really interact with him. Seeing him meant seeing my mother, and that was just something I wasn't too thrilled about. My mother had been clean for some time, but then she relapsed. My brother was going to be sent into foster care once CPS had discovered what was going on in their home. I knew that I couldn't allow that, so at 25, I became a full-time father to an eight-year-old boy.

Did I want to raise a kid at the prime time of my life, at 25 years old? Absolutely not. But the uncertainty and abuse that he could have endured in foster care was not something I ever wanted my brother to experience. He was not me. Looking back at all I'd accomplished to date, I can honestly say I defied a lot of odds. I became successful on my own—a self-made entrepreneur. I became a millionaire on my own. I became everything everybody said I couldn't be. I had everything stacked against me: foster kid, molestation, abuse, the product of a single mother household, victim of drugs, being shot, a victim of violent crime—I experienced everything everybody said would be the reason why somebody like me would not make it. I've overcome that, and I know it's because of God, right? My brother was not like me—I was always a strong, sharp kid. At six and seven I had a key to the house, and I was coming and going as I pleased. I was watching my younger sister, who was only three years old. I saw somebody get murdered. I was running the streets. I was living around dope. My brothers were dope boys. I grew up very differently than my little brother; he was very isolated and was a mama's boy. He was with her all the time. Not to mention, he had a lot of mental and developmental issues because my mother did drugs while she was pregnant with him. I look at foster care, and I didn't think my brother was strong enough to survive it.

Paul came to live with me, and it was during that time that I discovered that I wasn't the best parent. I didn't realize the effect that all the psychological and emotional abuse had on me until I was placed in a parental role. I didn't know how to be a good parent because I didn't have good parents. All I knew to do was discipline him when he did something wrong, or whoop his ass if he did something *really* wrong. If he did something good, I'd give him money or

138

buy him something. I didn't know how to love him. I don't think I knew how to love anyone. In some ways, having Paul with me was therapeutic. I didn't have the time to wallow in grief or lose myself in the bottom of the bottle because I had to be active and present for him each day. I had to be more responsible and level-headed because I was now his only parent.

I did try my best to be as close to a "normal" father for him as I could. I cooked at the house; we watched TV, played games, and rode around together. If any of the other kids tried to fuck with him, I'd be on their asses about it, or if I thought that something wasn't going right with his teachers, I'd advocate for him. I knew how to protect him because that's what my brother, Rodney, did for me. That's how he expressed his love for me, and because I didn't know many other expressions of love, protecting Paul was my best attempt.

I would pick him up from school or pick him up from my sister's house, who lived around the corner. I initiated awkward conversations about his day and listened to him tell me about things he liked:

"Hey, Jason!"

"Wassup."

"I was playing 'Space Rangers III' and I finally got to the next level!"

"Oh, that's dope."

"Yea, remember how Octon always uses his magma razor boom to hit you before you can get to the top of the building?"

"Umm...I think I remember something like that," I lied.

"I found out that if you press X and O a bunch of times there's a shield that comes out and it helps you finish the level!"

I didn't know what the fuck he was talking about sometimes, but I tried to listen.

I also didn't understand the challenges of raising a kid who had the issues that Paul had. Even though I put him in a good private school—the best private school that handled behavioral issues like his—and gave him the proper medications, took him to counseling all that, I know I didn't give him love because I didn't know how to do that. Then he just became difficult to care for. He had a lot of psychological issues and behavioral outbursts.

One morning, I was coming home from work, and as I was driving down the freeway, I saw a big cloud of black smoke coming from the area where I lived. At the time, my boyfriend, Josh, also lived with me, so I dialed him through my car's phone system and asked, "Where is my brother?"

"He's right here."

"Is there a fire?"

"Yeah, there's a fire outside," he confirmed.

"Okay. When was my brother outside?" I investigated. I don't know how, but I knew that Paul had to be involved in some way.

"Oh no," Josh defended Paul, "he wasn't outside."

I said, "No. Put him on the phone."

I waited for a few seconds and then heard Paul's nervous "Hello."

"Paul, did you go outside?"

"No, no, I didn't go outside," he lied.

"Okay, whatever. Put Josh back on the phone." Josh came back to the phone and he was wondering why I kept asking Paul's whereabouts. "Josh, did Paul go outside for *any* amount of time?"

He paused. "Well, he did go outside for about 15 minutes to walk the dog."

Boom. That's all I needed. Fifteen minutes was plenty of time for Paul to create chaos. Whatever was on fire, I knew he did it. That's just the type of person he had become. He was always involved in some shit. He was getting progressively worse, and then he started using drugs. When I got home, I was greeted by the police and the fire chief. My brother had been seen lighting a Molotov cocktail and throwing it across the street, onto the freeway. He lit the whole freeway and the palm trees across the street from the freeway on fire. There were helicopters dropping water, fire trucks, police officers, and all that. When I got to the house, I whooped his ass and told him, "You're on your way out of here. I've done everything I can. We drive in a Mercedes, you have clothes, you have your own room. You go to the best private school. You're traveling around the country with me. You have a good life."

The one thing I didn't realize until now is that maybe the lack of nurturing was more responsible for his behavior than his developmental issues. I just couldn't love him. I've decided not to be a parent because I know that I'm very selfish with my career right now, and I think I'm emotionally incapable of giving real genuine love to somebody. I haven't worked through all the issues that I need to work through to be able to be okay with that. I feel like when people get close to me or try to in a non-romantic way, I will immediately do everything to back away from that. It can be a family member or somebody wanting to be a real genuine friend—somebody who's genuinely just trying to get close to me. My brother never had a chance. I couldn't give him what he needed, and I wasn't patient with him.

After the Molotov cocktail incident, I called his social worker and told her, "Yeah, he gotta go." After Paul overheard the conversation, he jumped out of his bedroom window and went to the park next door. A family was there barbecuing, and he found their keys, went to the parking lot, and found their car. He stole the car, ended up crashing it, got arrested, and went to juvenile hall. I was done after that. I told the social worker again, "He can't come back to my house." That ended our 10-year relationship as "father" and "son."

Now that he's an adult, I rarely talk to him. Sadly, I don't talk to many of my family members. He'll call me when he needs something, and I'll make sure he's good. That's the totality of our relationship now—him calling when he needs something, and me helping him out when I can. I helped him get social security and gain a sense of financial security, but I boxed him out.

11

TOXIC ASS NIGGA

──────

E VERY NOW AND THEN, I would think about Calvin, but the reality was that we would never be together. We hadn't talked since the night he asked me to be his baby's godfather, and it was probably for the best. After Calvin and I broke up, Josh was my next serious relationship. I'll be honest: that relationship was just a good sexual relationship and was one that taught me what a relationship should never be like. It should never be about sex, and there were some things I knew I shouldn't have ever have tolerated.

I saw Josh on MySpace and we added each other. He was a boxer from the Bay area; I was living in LA at the time, so the distance was okay. We started communicating through MySpace, but I found out that he had a girlfriend. He wasn't the first guy I dated who had a girlfriend, and it wasn't an issue for me. If the guys had a girlfriend or a boyfriend, I didn't care; I was so destructive, that I didn't give a fuck about all that. I didn't give a fuck if you were straight or gay either. If I was interested and they seemed to be down, it went down. Josh and I talked regularly, and then I extended an invitation for us to meet in person.

"Yo, when I come up here, I'm going to meet you."

He was like, "Okay, cool."

Shortly after that conversation, I bought a new Mercedes. I didn't even want to go to sleep because it was my first Mercedes. I called Josh and said, "Hey, I'm going to drive up to get you from the Bay area and then I want you to come stay with me for a week."

He was like, "Okay, cool. Shit, I'm down. Whatever." At the time he was living with his girl and her kids, but he didn't give a fuck.

I drove to where he was, and he was spending so much time wondering what he should pack. I was like, "Don't pack shit, we'll get all your clothes and a toothbrush. Just get in the car." He was feeling that. He got in the car, and then we headed to LA. Within that week's time, we became friendly. We had already been talking, so it wasn't like it was a surprise that there was a sexual interest. What surprised me was that he had actually messed around with men before. Once we got to the house and we started hanging out, we found out really quickly that we were sexually compatible. He was a freak, much to my enjoyment.

Around this time, my job was transferring me to Stockton, so I made a bold suggestion.

"Fuck it, just come move in with me."

"Fuck it," Josh agreed. "What about my girl?"

"Man, for real?" I dismissed him. "Just kill that shit. You don't want her anyway."

He went home where his woman was living, got all his things, got in the car, and moved in with me. It was the craziest thing, but the spontaneity of it all was exhilarating. I bought a four-bedroom, four-bathroom two-story house and we moved in together, along with my little brother, Paul (before I kicked him out). I bought the house directly across the street from my job just so I could go home and have sex during lunch. We were having sex probably four times a day when we first got together. It was insane.

The relationship was good sexually, but I allowed that to be the determining factor of our overall compatibility. The first conversation I had with him once we decided to be together was very simple but it was the foundation that I needed to establish with him.

"There are three things that I don't tolerate in a relationship: don't cheat on me, don't lie to me, and don't steal from me. Everything else, we can work through. If there is poor communication, or you don't clean the house, or I don't, or we forget to pay a bill, we can work through that. Even if we get in a crazy argument, that's workable."

The longer I was with Josh, the more I realized that he had some cognitive challenges. I don't think he was 100% mentally competent. He presented like he did, but there were times when he would have different types of cognitive breaks. I could tell there were other elements causing his reactions to certain things. Then I found out that his mother tried to drown him when he was a kid, so that did some damage to his brain.

After we were together three months, our first major challenge as a couple presented itself. I was going to purchase a few computers from a lady, but I wouldn't be in town to do the transaction. I looked to Josh to take care of things while I was away.

"Ok, she's going to sell these computers at $500 dollars each," I filled him in. "Here's $1500; I'll just get three of them. I've got to go to Puerto Rico for work, so when I get back, I'll check the computers out to make sure they're good."

I went to Puerto Rico and then returned shortly after. I bought all types of gifts and clothes and was anxious to show Josh what I had. When I inquired about the computer transaction, I noticed that there was only one computer.

"Where's the change?" I inquired. "You know, $1000."

"Oh, well..." I watched intently as Josh stumbled through his lie. "I lost the money."

"How did you lose the money? Did you go anywhere this weekend?"

"No, I didn't go anywhere."

I paused and tried to process what was happening. I just knew he didn't think I was stupid or that I would be okay with him just "losing" a grand.

"Did anybody come to the house?" I tried to bail him out.

"No."

At the time, my little brother was still living with me, so I said, "So you were home with Josh and you didn't leave the house?"

"No."

"And nobody came over?"

"No."

I could feel my anger erupting. "But you lost the $1000?"

He looked me square in the eye and confirmed, "Yeah."

"Well, that doesn't even fucking make sense, my nigga. Like, how did you lose the money and you didn't go nowhere? How did somebody not take the money, and you claim nobody came in the house?"

He stood there like I was talking to someone else.

"Look, I'm just going to tell you right now: I'm too smart for this conversation, and $1000 is not worth us continuing to argue. I'm going to go ahead and just chalk it up to the game, but I know this shit is funny. It's going to come out."

So, of course, being the freaks that we were, we got past the argument and had sex. While Josh was in the shower, I went to check my computer. I always kept my desktop organized, so when I turned it on, I immediately noticed a new icon that wasn't there before. I'm thinking, *What the fuck is this?* I clicked the box, and it was a video. I played the video, and there was Josh dancing and stripping for somebody while he was in my house. Somebody else was filming him.

He was still in the shower, so I kept my cool. When he finally came back in the room, I light-heartedly said, "Yo, I'm about to show you something. Before I show you, I need you to just remain calm and let me just show you this. Then we're going to talk about it." I played the video, and he immediately got defensive.

"Oh, so dancing," he shrugged. I could tell that he was trying hard to make this seem like it was nothing.

"Hold on a minute," I continued. "So now either, A, my brother was filming you, and that's a fucking problem, or, B, somebody was in my house filming you, and that's a problem. So ..."

Then he lashed out, "You work too much and I'm home alone! You travel all the time, so what am I supposed to do? I met this girl at the park, and she came over!" He admitted that he had cheated on me with her.

"Okay." I thought very carefully about how I was going to respond. Instead of saying, "You violated my trust, stole my money, cheated on me, and you lied to me," I accepted what he did. Instead of saying, "You know what? This relationship is over and you're out," I stayed in that relationship for another two and a half years. Even though I stayed, the relationship quickly went downhill. I spent the rest of our relationship cheating and sleeping with whoever I wanted. Our relationship had become so disrespectful and toxic that there was one time when I was about to sleep with someone and, I found out that Josh had already slept with him *in our bed*. Come to find out later, he and Calvin used to mess around, too. They weren't even in a serious dating relationship; it was strictly sexual. I didn't find that out until later, but it was something that made me uneasy.

The relationship was clearly in critical condition, and our move to LA finally gave me what I needed to pull the plug. My job promoted me to director, and that position was in LA. Despite the relationship being toxic, I asked Josh to move with me. Being in LA afforded me the opportunity to be more active in the entertainment industry, and I started to develop relationships with a few celebrities. I could sense that Josh was becoming more and more insecure. While we were out for drinks with a few friends, he got too drunk and spazzed out and left. When he got home, I got a phone call from my brother telling me to come back to the house.

"Hey, you need to come home. Josh just broke the doorknob, and he just punched the kitchen window. He punched a hole in my bedroom door, too."

"What? Put him on the phone!" I knew Josh wouldn't talk, so I left and came home. When I got home, I ran up the stairs and encountered a drunk, belligerent Josh.

"Fuck your motherfuckin' ass, Jason!" he shouted. Then something hard flew past my face.

149

"Nigga, you betta calm the fuck down!" I shouted back. "You in here fucking up my house like you ain't got no goddamn sense! What the fuck is wrong with you?"

"You ain't shit!" he retorted.

"Yo, you gotta get out my house."

He got in my face and yelled, "Make me, motherfucker!" I blacked out. There was more screaming and cursing, and the next thing I knew, we were in a full-on fight. I was on top of him whooping his ass. I was throwing blows and he was giving them back. He reached up to grab my hair, which was a lot longer back then, and there was blood everywhere. Once I saw all the blood, my anger subsided, and I realized what I was doing. I was really hurting him. I had never been in a physically abusive relationship with anybody I was intimate with. I didn't know how to classify what was happening. *Is this domestic violence? Is this just a fight?* We were both men, so it could have been seen as just two guys fighting, but this was my partner, so I guess it was domestic violence.

I just blacked the fuck out. I knew that I could not allow my rage to take over me like that, and I knew that I could not be in a relationship that was steeped in violence and betrayal. I knew that the relationship was over. I had to be. I had to end the relationship because he didn't deserve what happened, and it wasn't wise for me to remain in a situation where I can't control myself. I know the extent of my rage, and that's why I don't own a gun today. I know how I am, and in that relationship, I knew that if I didn't end it, I could have eventually killed him.

We sat down together and came up with a 30-day plan for us to transition out of the relationship. It was enough time for him to find somewhere else to live. I didn't know who I had become while in the relationship with Josh, but I won't say that it was only because of him. I'm grateful for the time I spent with Josh because I learned a few things: I deserve someone who was straight up with me, and I did not want to be in a dysfunctional relationship. I took him, his luggage, and our dog and dropped them off at the bus and got him a one-way ticket back to northern California. I haven't talked to him or seen him since. I don't even know where he is, but I wish him all the best in his endeavors.

***

At some point during the tenure of my relationship with Josh, I rekindled my friendship with Calvin. We both had other relationships since we'd been together, but there was no bad blood. He was dating a guy named T, and we all got along pretty well. Whatever crazy, cool experience I was having, I wanted him to partake, and the night I got invited to Prince's after-party in 2011 was one of those times.

I was in New York, and a friend of mine took me over to Melyssa Ford's house. He introduced me to Melyssa and she casually mentioned that she had tickets to the Prince concert and that she was going that night. I grinned. I loved Prince. I've dressed up like him for Halloween and had *Purple Rain* on repeat. Ever since those mini-concerts I would have as a six-year-old in my living room, I had always appreciated his artistry. Melyssa asked us if we wanted to go, and we were all over it.

We went to Madison Square Garden, and while we were sitting in our seats, Steven Hill, who was the president of BET at the time, walked toward us. Melyssa had been on BET, so when he saw her, he said, "Why aren't you guys down by the stage?"

She said, "We don't have any passes to get down there." Steven gave us some purple bands, and then we headed down to the stage. We were sharing space with Jimmy Fallon, Mos Def, Questlove, and a bunch of other celebrities. It was really intimate yet overwhelming.

I saw Miguel, who I knew, sitting in the audience across the stage, and then the stage manager came over and said, "You guys want to get up on stage?"

We gave him a unanimous, "Hell yeah!" We got up on stage and danced with Prince. The stage was built like his infamous symbol, and his dancers were dancing on skates while he was going around the stage playing the guitar. Questlove got on the drums, Jimmy Fallon got a guitar while Mos Def, A. J. Calloway and I were just standing there watching all this shit go down. It was crazy.

I didn't care what I was doing or what anybody else thought of me; I had the opportunity to share a stage with an icon. It was electric. I was a grown man, but that little boy was leaping to come out and take center-stage. I thought he had died, but that night showed me that he was still alive. I cherished that night because even though that experience was brief, it gave me back that careless light-hearted spirit that life had tried its best to snuff out.

After the performance, Miguel walked over to me while we were on stage and said, "Hey, Prince just invited us to his private after-party. You can come." The party was at a little club—it was a very intimate space. There was someone performing on stage, and I became star-struck by all the celebrities I saw there: Leonardo Di-Caprio, Jay-Z, Madonna ... I had to share this moment with someone else, and since Calvin lived in New York, I called him immediately.

"Yo, you need to come down to this club!" I pretended to panic. "I'm about to get jumped; these guys are trying to get me." I knew if I had told him the real reason why I wanted him to come he would have chickened out.

"I'm on my way, and I'm bringing T!"

Calvin and T pulled up like the getaway drivers of a bank robbery because they thought I was about to get jumped. Calvin called me and asked, "Are we at the right place? There are a lot of police out here, and there are barricades. We can't even get in the club."

"No, you at the right spot. I was lying, let me come outside." I went out there and I got them. I brought Calvin in, and Calvin looked at me like he wanted to punch me.

"Yo, you got us thinking some shit was going down!"

I said, "Nah, it's cool." I was trying to act nonchalant because I knew that he was getting ready to lose his mind.

When we walked in, Calvin was checking the place out, and then he looked at the table where Miguel and Melyssa Ford were sitting.

He paused and said, "Is that Miguel?"

I'm like, "Yeah, yeah, yeah."

He looked at me and said, "What the fuck is this?"

"Come with me to the bathroom. I'm about to tell you where we at." Calvin and I walked toward the bathroom, and Leonardo DiCaprio walked by. Calvin gasped and said, "Yo, son, is that Leonard DiCaprio? Oh, shit!" I was trying to get him to calm the fuck down, but because Calvin didn't live his life working with celebrities, he was psyched.

Calvin lived in Brooklyn and is a huge Jay-Z fan. We were getting closer to the bathroom and we passed by Jay-Z's table. He yelled, "You got to be fucking kidding me."

I'm like, "Yeah, yeah, yeah, that's Jay-Z." We finally made it to the bathroom, and I started explaining. "Okay, listen. This is Prince's private party, nigga. I don't know how we got in here, but we in here. I just didn't want to experience this shit by myself, but—"

"Prince is here?" he shrieked.

"Oh, yeah," I responded nonchalantly like I wasn't just about to have a whole fit while I was on stage with him. We walked out, and as soon as we turn the corner, Prince was sitting there with Madonna. When Calvin first got to the club, he ordered some bottles, but after he saw Prince and Madonna, he was so overwhelmed by it all, he just left. He couldn't even stand to be in the building.

I called him, like, "Nigga, you got to come back and pay for these bottles." Nobody just orders bottles and leaves. I was like, *What the fuck?* He regained his composure and came back. We paid for the bottles, we got drunk, and we had a good time. There was no arguing or no conversations about unrequited love. I'm glad that the foundation of our relationship was strong enough for us to still remain friends.

12

TRAYVON MARTIN AND ACTIVISM

TO KEEP THE BILLS PAID, I had immersed myself in work. Though I was around celebrities, I wasn't one—I still needed to make a constant income. I was still trying to determine who I was and what I had to offer the world, and navigating in that space was always eventful. The death of Whitney Houston and all the issues that had arisen from caused me to take a break from events and I decided to get back to my grassroots in youth advocacy. I had lost a great role model, Ed Fleming, but I didn't lose the love that I had for youth which he allowed me to discover when I worked as a youth counselor. Shortly after, I worked in the probation department because I really wanted to help at-risk kids. After a few months on the job, I discovered that the system wasn't really interested in helping those kids succeed; it was a business. I ended up encountering a lot of racism and a lot of politics, so I became an advocate for the kids. Despite my primary responsibility of being a probation officer, I felt like my first job was to do whatever I could to help them make it. I was once a kid in the system, and I had to do most of my own advocating.

I ended up filing a complaint with the juvenile justice commissioner about how some of the staff were abusing the kids. On Halloween, they gathered the kids from the low-security section and dressed them up like Jason from *Friday the 13th*. The staff forced them to put on orange jumpsuits and ski masks, and then they handcuffed and shackled them and walked them around from unit to unit. They would just make a big joke of it all and take pictures and laugh hysterically. The kids were forced to participate against their will, and that pissed me off that they weren't treated with dignity. To add to an already fucked up situation, the staff would frequently refer to some of the kids as "niggers." Here I was, a Black man, and they didn't even respect me enough to at least not use that word in my presence! On top of that, I knew that the administration had purposely passed me up for a promotion even though I had the highest scores on my tests and had the best experience for the position. Guess they just didn't want a Black man as an authority figure in the criminal justice system.

They found out about my complaint and fired me. I ended up suing them and then became an advocate in the community. The union was already aware of my advocacy and what I was going through because they were representing me. The day after I got fired, I was hired with the union and became one of the realest, most respected union leaders within the industry of labor, the labor movement. I did that for 10 years and became a staff director over Kaiser Permanente in California. Then I became a regional director, so I had statewide responsibilities.

Eventually, the union was taken over by our parent union because we were using the members' dues to fight some disparities within the union. Somehow that was a violation of the rules, so we all ended up losing our jobs. The president and all the executives ended up getting removed, and all of us secondary leaders were all corralled into rooms at a hotel. We had to go through an interview process with the parent-union to be rehired. We had to explain our loyalty to them, and we had to agree to lie to the members.

I had a decision to make: was I going to lie and lose all my integrity with these people and keep a really good job, or was I going to quit and figure out life? It was an easy decision: I quit and joined the opposing union, the National Union of Healthcare Workers (NUHW). While I was there, we organized the members to leave; we got 91,000 out of over 100,000 members to sign a petition to leave the union within 10 days.

I worked at NUHW for about a year, and then I joined the California Nursing Association. I lost my passion for the labor movement because it became all about politics and less about the people. I left that career path behind, and I really started hustling. I started to make friends with different people in the entertainment industry and started to offer consulting services or party promotion, but I still had a heart for my community. I had acquired all of these skills within the labor union and I wanted to use them to make a difference.

One day while I was back home in Stockton visiting family, I was watching the news and saw that five kids were shot in their backyard during a graduation celebration. I was just so shocked that that was still happening. The city had literally become as dangerous as it was in '97 when my brother was murdered. I got in the car. I drove down to city hall, and I asked to speak to the mayor. When she came out, I asked her, "What is going on in this city?" I needed to know what her plan was to protect the people. My niece was entering kindergarten, and I was really concerned about how unsafe the city was. I didn't want her or any other kid to have his or her life cut short because of the violence that dominated Stockton. Then I started looking at what was happening in the community at large, and I immersed myself into the city's restoration. I actually moved home for three months to put together a plan. I organized the community to talk about safety and accountability, and I started this whole initiative called "I Am Ready," which was about youth empowerment and leadership and safety.

In taking that meeting and then going on to do that initiative, I started meeting with community leaders, union leaders, drug dealers, fucking gangbangers—I was meeting with everybody. City council, the mayor, Congressmen, the Senator. At that time, there was a national conversation going on about gun violence as it related to the Trayvon Martin case. I was compelled to meet with Trayvon's older brother, Jahavaris, because I knew what he was going through. I lived with the pain of losing Rodney, so I just wanted to support Jahavaris and the rest of the family the best way I could. My attorney reached out to Trayvon Martin's attorney, Ben Crump, and I flew to New York and met with Trayvon's mother. I got her permission to team up, and we created a campaign to bring awareness to the Trayvon Martin case.

We created the official Trayvon Martin T-shirt and officially launched the campaign. I had worked for the union, so my experience there was helpful in thoroughly and properly creating a campaign. We also created a website and arranged for a bunch of celebrities to take photos in this shirt and post it on their social to raise awareness. We get everybody from Chris Brown to Matt Barnes, and Tank. We asked our personal connections to participate and even had Omarosa lend her support. I flew to Miami and I shot Trayvon's entire family in the shirt. That was a special moment for me because they trusted me with handling Trayvon's memory. They trusted my vision and supported me even though they were heart-broken and grief-stricken. They let me in, as a result, we raised a lot of awareness and participated in the conversation about gun-violence and police brutality within the African American community. We wanted to there to be a world-wide concentration on gun laws and the lack of protections for people of color, and more specifically, the effect that Trayvon's murder and other murders like them have on communities.

***

I wanted to make a bigger impact in the lives of people around me, and that opportunity came to me in the form of a 17-year-old boy named Jaelyn Bague. Jaelyn reached out to me on Facebook and told me that he was a fan of mine. He said that he had a rap group and that he really wanted to meet me. I didn't know that I had "fans" and I was flattered that he thought I was someone he could look up to. I remembered when I got that phone call from Michael Jackson when I was around his age, and although I wasn't on Michael's level, if I could have given another kid a fraction of the excitement I felt that day, I was willing. When I went to his page, I scrolled through his pictures and was taken aback by how much he looked just like me. It was crazy. I got an eerie feeling because I thought about how much I had looked like Ed back when he mentored me. When I did more digging, I found out that I had gone to school with his dad, and I knew his mom.

I responded to his message and said, "Okay, when I come home to Stockton, I'll reach out to you and your co-rapper. I'll get with both of you, and then we'll meet up."

I made good on my word, and the next time I was in Stockton, we linked up. He introduced me to the newest city council member, Michael Tubbs, who happened to be the youngest Black man elected to the city council. He was a big deal and was even endorsed by Oprah.

Jaelyn and I became great friends. When I did the tribute to Whitney Houston on the anniversary of her death, I invited Jaelyn to come along. I knew that Dana would be there and he had mentioned before how much he loved Queen Latifah, so I wanted to introduce them.

Sometime during the evening, I had Jaelyn follow me to where Dana was and I said, "Hey, Dana, this is Jaelyn. He's from Stockton, and he's a rapper. Don't he look just like me?"

She laughed and said, "Yeah, he does. Nice to meet you Jaelyn." He gave her a hug and then she turned to me and said, "I hope you're doing for him what I did for you." That stuck with me. It was my responsibility to pay it forward. As much as I reached forward, I needed to reach back.

***

Though I was doing everything I could to bring comfort and support to the Martin/Fulton family and trying my best to pour into Jaelyn, the relationships with my own family members were still damaged. I could have literally killed my father. Talking about Trayvon no doubt stirred up a lot of emotions about Rodney, and I was angry with my father because of our interactions after Rodney was killed. He was very insensitive. My brother was a drug dealer at the time, and after he died, my father stole two kilos of Rodney's stash, sold it, and didn't give any money to Rodney's daughter. Then he took all Rodney's property and distributed it out to his brothers and other people.

Rodney also had an old school car that he had worked on; he was so proud of it. He painted it red (because he was a Blood) and customized the interior with red and white seats. He put a lot of money and work into it. My dad gave it to his brother, my uncle Ricky, who my brother was never even close to. They had no relationship. He may have even sold it to him. If he did, he definitely kept all the money.

He didn't even give anything to us as a keepsake. He was very selfish; he was divisive. He wasn't a person who brought the family together. He's an elderly man now, and I'm not sure that he is any different than he was when we were just dealing with Rodney's death.

We've only had one conversation about Rodney, and it was terrible. About fifteen years had passed since Rodney died, and I thought that we'd be able to talk about it as sensible, mature adults, but the conversation ended up being a heated, bitter discussion. Rodney's murder came up when I was back home working on the Trayvon Martin campaign with Trayvon's family. I was also continuing to do work in the community as a mentor, and I took Jaelyn to my dad's house with me because I had a meeting with Ralph White, a well-known community leader, who happened to be a friend of my dad's.

During our meeting at Ralph's house, a local pastor told me that some community leaders were up in arms because I was doing so much to organize the city. I don't know why anyone would have been upset because things definitely needed to change in Stockton. I continued to meet with a lot of different groups within the city, I was learning and strategizing how to bring change. I had been meeting with Ralph White; he was like the one Black guy in Stockton who everybody listened to because he had been very successful. He had been on the city council, but it was also rumored that he was corrupt.

As our meeting continued, the pastor went on to say, "You over here talking about this and that. You ain't even from Stockton. You from LA. You don't know nothing about violence in Stockton."

I was so offended by him acting like he knew me, so I clapped back. "Nigga, I've been shot in Stockton! I've walked these Stockton streets all my life! My brother was murdered in Stockton! Don't talk to me about violence in Stockton. I'm a product of the violence in Stockton."

I was getting ready to leave and then my father chimed in, "Well, you know we got to learn how to forgive people just like you got to learn how to forgive the woman who killed your brother."

I had never had a conversation with him about any of the things that he did or any of the ways he behaved afterward. His comment caught me off guard, and the mood of the room immediately changed. My other brother, Link, was also there sitting with his wife. He had his own issues because he and Rodney were at odds before Rodney died, and they never got the chance to make up. While Rodney was in prison, he trusted Link to oversee a drug deal for him. Instead of Link giving the money to Rodney's girl, he kept it all. He didn't look out for her. Rodney found out and promised to kill Link when he got out, but he went to prison right when Rodney got out. That guilt was brewing.

Jaelyn and my stepmom were sitting there, and my niece was playing on the floor. Rodney has always been a hot spot for me, so I couldn't let that pass.

"Nigga, what did you just say?" I didn't care about him speaking on forgiveness because I felt he had no right to say anything about Rodney being killed. He was a shitty father after it all went down. His comment sent me into a rage.

"What?" he responded flatly.

I repeated myself, "What the fuck did you just say?"

"You need to watch your mouth," my father warned.

"Nigga, I'll beat your fucking ass!" I would've, too. I was ready for anything after that. "Don't ever bring my brother's name up. Don't ever say nothing about him. Don't ever speak on his name."

My father was saying something else to me, but I blacked out. I didn't care about anything else he had to say, and I continued.

"The way you shitted on him when he died—the way you took all his shit and treated his house like a fucking garage sale! Literally letting people come in and take whatever they want! You sold his stuff *and* took his dope and sold it in the hood and didn't take nothing to his kids or nothing."

Then he jumped up, "Well you didn't even come to the courthouse when she was sentenced for his murder!"

"What the fuck are you talking about? I was there from day one! I was there! Every day I was there when she went to trial. And

I was there when she was sentenced—I spoke at her sentencing! What the fuck are you talking about?"

Then Link interjected, "Hold on, hold on."

I immediately snapped at him next. "And you! What the fuck are you talking about? No, *you* hold on. You were in fucking prison. Did he save the car for you? Did he at least save something for you?"

Link was a Blood, too, so it would have been fitting if my dad gave Rodney's car to Link.

"Did he at least save something for you like a memento? Did he at least think about you and giving you something? Did he think about giving it to me? Did he think about giving it to somebody who actually was close to him, so we would have a keepsake? Nah!"

I turned my attention back to my father, "Nigga, you fucking shitted on my brother." Then I told Link, "And you're going to sit up here and stick up for this nigga? Don't fucking tell me shit." I had never argued with Link like that before.

It was a very tense environment, and Link's wife started crying. She knew that this was out of my character and I was never the guy to talk crazy. Before then, I never talked crazy to my dad. He was my dad. It was just something I knew not to do. I didn't have that type of relationship with him. We'd usually just talk in passing or kind of shoot the shit talking, but we never had an intense father/son moment. I was releasing a lot of pent up anger, and I continued.

"At my mom's funeral you tapped me on my shoulder and had the nerve to ask me what her last name was like she wasn't shit to

167

you. The mother of your child. You've been a disrespectful nigga forever, and I've always respected you in spite of it."

I was unloading on him. I paused for a moment and tried to gather myself. Then I looked at his wife and felt sorry for her, but I had more to say.

"And you been cheating on her your whole fucking marriage to her. You ain't loyal to nobody. You don't give a fuck about nobody. You cheated on her your whole marriage. You have all these kids with all these different women. You've *been* disrespecting her."

His wife looked at me feeling a sense of vindication because somebody was talking about it. Finally.

"Don't ever speak to me about my brother. Ever."

I flipped that meeting up-side-down. My mentee was sitting like, "What the fuck is going on?" He couldn't leave. He couldn't even move. I was crying, and my sister-in-law was still crying. I went off on my brother again, but he didn't say anything because he knew that everything I was saying was true. My dad was trying to defend himself, but I wouldn't allow it.

"No, nigga, you not getting out of this conversation. You're not getting a pass." One thing that I'm protective of is my brother's memory. His life is important to me. I'm not going to let anybody shit on him, not even in death.

13

MEETING FLOYD MAYWEATHER

N ATURALLY, I WAS PISSED at Link, and I missed Rodney terribly.
I took all that anger and constant grief and channeled it into my
career as a blogger. In 2011, Rob Kardashian and I were hanging out,
and I was straight up with him about making some real moves: "Bro,
we need to figure out a way to make some money." After that conversation, I created a company called "the Conglomerate Group,"
which was a consulting company that offered creative services. I
started working with Rob on his foundation in the entertainment
industry. Then I started my personal blog called "Low-
KeyMessy.Com," and it scared the shit out of people. People knew
and trusted me, and I was around so many people intimately that
when I launched LowKeyMessy.com, people were afraid that I would
expose some of their deepest darkest secrets. My idea was to be

funny, light-hearted, but "messy." I didn't want it to be disastrous to anyone's career like an exposé. People didn't really understand the branding of it all, and so I quickly strategized and rebranded.

One night, I had dinner with Alex Avant, the son of Clarence Avant. He kept asking me, "How would you market this product, or how would you market this or that..." I kept naming people I'd call to endorse what I was doing, and then Alex gave me the foundation for who I am as a brand today.

"Stop talking about what you would do with other people. Like how would you do it *yourself*? You're a brand." I couldn't see myself as a brand because coming from the labor industry as a union brat, I was conditioned to be selfless. It wasn't about us; it was always about the work. The union was never about trying to be in front or taking credit for anything, it was always about being in the back. It was hard for me to see myself as a brand. Alex went on, "The problem with you is that you are the Jack of All Trades, but you master nothing. People just know you and they know you can do it all, but nobody knows that you're the go-to guy for one thing." I had no brand identity.

The next day after my meeting with Alex, Queen Latifah called me. We were having a random conversation, and she mentioned that she had run into Perez Hilton in New York. She said, "You know what? You remind me of him, but you're more like a TMZ and Perez but with a heart." I really took that in. I looked up to Perez because his career has always inspired me to do what I do. "You really need to focus on that," she continued. "That's your lane. That's you."

"It's so crazy," I lit up, "because I just had this dinner where somebody was telling me that!"

I immediately rebranded my LowKeyMessy site. I just deleted it. I was so mad because I spent $5,000 dollars to create. In its place I created "IAmJasonLee.Com" and my tagline was "Hollywood Unlocked." I wrote about what was happening in pop culture, events I was going to, shoes that I liked, and music that I liked. People really started liking it, and it gained some popularity, but it still wasn't quite what I wanted it to be. I was going to quit the industry altogether because I was so frustrated that the site wasn't bringing in the revenue I wanted. I was making money doing all types of other side hustles.

***

I was still finding ways to strategize and propel my career and I happened to be at a party at David Banner's house with Chris Brown and Karrueche. I had just introduced them, but while at David's house, I saw someone who I knew I needed to have. His name is Lature, and my initial draw to him was how fine he was. He was light skin with tattoos all over his athletic body. He was about six feet and he looked like a model. I walked up to him and asked for his number, and we ended up hanging out the next day.

Although I wanted to pursue him romantically, Lature's intentions were different. He wanted our lunch date to be a networking opportunity. I was so drunk at the party that I forgot I even had his number. He had to remind me that we were supposed to meet up that day, and when he sent me his picture to remind me, I made sure

171

I connected with him. We sat at the table together and I was overtly flirting with him and trying to convince him to go out with me. He told me he had never been with a man and that he had no desire to do so. I was still clear with him that I didn't want to network with him, that I wanted him, and that I wanted to be with him. I don't know what it was, but something in me told me that he was going to be mine.

Over the next year and a half, we would still connect and hang out. He still insisted that he just wanted to be friends, but I maintained how I felt about him. We would text each other often and sometimes run into each other at clubs—he would always be friendly but be careful not to lead me on. I was living in Hollywood for a while and hadn't realized how toxic my environment was. I had gotten so caught up with my surroundings that I didn't even realize that I was changing and losing myself. Lature was an escape from the superficiality and judgment that would sometimes come with the Hollywood scene. He was from Houston, and he was very grounded and normal. I felt completely comfortable around him, and I really liked him.

Eventually, with us growing closer and spending more time together, Lature told me that he was open to seeing where the vibe went between us. The vibe was so good that we decided to pursue a relationship and move in together pretty quickly. Before we got together, he was a local promoter, but as our relationship progressed, he went from being the guy who opened the rope for people to sitting at the owner's table. His life changed.

Then my life, that was somewhat chaotic and out of control, became more balanced and more organized because of him. It was a great relationship. It was the first relationship I had been in where I really felt that there was a lot of real love, honesty, and loyalty—he was the complete opposite of Joshua. We were able to make a lot of money together and be successful together. At one point, we started a business that generated about $10,000 a day. With all the money we were making, it was easy to be frivolous: somebody would say, "Yo, let's go to Vegas, let's go to Miami, let's head to London or Paris," but Lature would shut it down and tell me to put the money in the bank. We had a great balance: I was the one who could go out and figure out how to make all the money, and he kept the household balanced. Shit, he kept my *life* balanced.

***

As I continued to make connections, I was fortunate enough to be in a position to be mentored by Floyd Mayweather. I was familiar with Floyd's career, but he piqued my attention when he posted a rather personal picture on his social media pages regarding the reason for his breakup with his fiancé. There was a lot going on with him and his brand due to the nature of the post, and I had experience consulting and branding.

His assistant, Kitchie, who I had known for a long time, invited me to come to Vegas during the fight weekend, and she said, "I want you to meet Floyd because I know you know everybody."

I was an aspiring blogger at the time with my personal blog; it wasn't a real legitimate brand and it wasn't really making me money.

Nonetheless, she knew I knew everybody, and she knew I was really smart when it came to dealing with content online.

I flew to Vegas and stayed in a crappy hotel over the weekend. I was supposed to meet up with them on Friday, but I didn't hear anything. Saturday came, and there was nothing. When Sunday came I got nervous because I still didn't hear anything and my flight was supposed to leave that day.

I texted Kitchie and said, "Hey, I'm going home."

She replied, "No, come to this address," and then she texted me Floyd's mother's home address. I got a Taxi and rushed over to his mom's house.

When I arrived, Kitchie didn't delay introducing me to Floyd:

"Hey, Floyd, this is Jason Lee, and he's a blogger."

Floyd said, "Oh, okay. Well, nice to meet you. Bring him to the Big Boy Mansion." The Big Boy Mansion was what Floyd named his house. We headed there and I was in company with Flo Rida, Katt Williams among others.

He had a ritual after every fight: he would go to his mother's house and watch his fight playback. People would eat, drink, play cards, talk, or whatever else—the house was usually full of family, friends, a few celebrities, and people who were close to Floyd.

While I was at the Big Boy Mansion, Floyd came up to me in the middle of the room while everybody looked on and said, "So, tell me about you."

I said, "I'm a blogger, and I'm gay."

Everybody, including Floyd, looked shocked. He chuckled and said, "Why would you say that?"

I said, "Well, because if you can accept me for who I am, then cool. If not, this shit doesn't really matter to me because I don't really know you. I mean, it is what it is."

Then he was like, "Well, I'm cool. I don't have any friends—any male friends—who are gay."

"No," I interjected, "I been here for a little bit. You *definitely* have a male friend who's gay."

He fell out laughing, and he grabbed my arm and pulled me outside. He was still laughing hysterically, and he was like, "Who, *him*?" Then he pointed out one of his friends.

I smiled and said, "Yeah, he gay."

He fell out laughing again, and from there, we sat down. He sat across from me and initiated a conversation. "Okay, so you a blogger, huh?" He crossed his arms curiously and said, "Okay, so ask me any question you want."

I perked up. "Okay, I don't know much about you, but everybody says that you running from Pacquiao—what's up with that?"

He was taken aback that I asked him that question directly. He sat at the edge of his seat and said, "Okay, let me break it down." During that conversation, he poured everything out. He told me about his marketing strategy, his childhood, how he was poor, and how he's suffered from parents who had drug addictions, like mine. He went to go stay with another family, like I did, and he told me about how he came from poverty and came from an impoverished community. He said that he built his massive brand by locking into his passion, and then working hard and staying dedicated.

Then he talked about how a white family had taken care of him, how he was robbed at the Olympics, and when I really listened to what fueled his passion, I discovered that it was people not believing in him, and him believing in himself.

So back to Pacquiao: Floyd shared how that once world said that Manny Pacquiao was the one person that could beat him, he decided that he was going to make Manny the last person he fought. He said that he would always have a reason for people to hate him, but he would continue to make hundreds of millions of dollars fighting these people.

Then he pulled out a huge diamond ring and a few watches. He laid everything on the table and asked me, "What are you doing?"

I told him, "I'm an aspiring blogger," and told him all the plans that I had for my brand. "But I was going to actually quit tomorrow, and just go back to work, because I've tried. I've gone everywhere I can go, and this shit just isn't working, so maybe it's not meant to be."

Floyd looked at me and then pulled out a check for 42 million dollars. He said, "This is why you don't quit. You're the Floyd Mayweather of media, and I can tell that if you just apply yourself and focus, you'll become bigger than you can ever expect." I really felt that.

I went home on fire. I told Lature about my talk with Floyd. He was excited because he knew who Floyd was. I had a new surge of energy and I met with my team as soon as I could. I started to evaluate how to restructure all of my business and shift gears. I knew that Floyd would be in DC hosting an event for a foundation, so I told Lature, "Yo, we're going to fly to DC and to support Floyd, and I want you to meet him."

We flew to DC and his assistant told me what hotel they were staying at. Floyd didn't know I was coming, and when he got out the car, there was paparazzi, security, and fans everywhere. He saw me, looked around puzzled, and immediately made an opening through the crowd. He walked over to Lature and me, and said, "Yo, what you doing here?"

I said, "I came out here to support you."

"For real?" he said. "How you get here?"

I said, "We flew ourselves."

"Really?" he was surprised.

"Yeah." I pointed to Lature and said, "This my nigga right here."

Floyd said, "Oh, what's up, homie?" Then he dapped him up.

I said, "No, this is my *nigga*. Like this is the person I sleep with every night."

He was like, "Oh, for real?"

177

I really liked Floyd. I liked what he stood for and I enjoyed learning more about his story. I regarded him in the same way that I regarded Rodney—that bigger brother figure, that person giving good advice, or that mentor. I really felt something special with Floyd the first day I met him, but I needed to know that this was going to be a real relationship. The litmus test of the relationship was Floyd knowing who I was and accepting that. There's a lot of testosterone around The Money Team, except for the strippers, so I wasn't going to let them be any different with me.

Floyd met Lature, and we went up to the room. He was pacing the room with his arms crossed, trying to figure how to ask the questions, so I said, "Let's just get right to all the questions you have because I know you have questions." Floyd just started laughing

"Okay," he began. "So you're gay."

Lature said, "No."

Floyd blinked and looked more confused than he had ever been. "Wait a minute, but you in a relationship with him?"

"Yes."

"But you're not gay."

"No."

Then we started a whole conversation about how Lature was still attracted to women, and by the end of it, Floyd was baffled. He also found it really humorous and he said, "I really like you. Let's get

you some TMT clothes." He turned to his assistant
Jason that rainbow shirt, the rainbow TMT shirt."

I said, "Nigga, I don't wear rainbow. What tl
lutely didn't wear rainbow. "All gay people don't wear rainbows an
the time!" Everybody found humor in that, but what I saw looking
back was, after everything that happened that weekend, he put me
on the jet, and he gave me all his phone numbers.

His assistant was like, "He don't ever invite nobody on the jet
that ain't a part of the team, and he don't give nobody these direct
lines. He clearly trusts you and gets good vibes from you."

***

He flew me to Vegas and put me up. We went out later that
night, and at 3:00 in the morning, a guy took a video of him. Floyd
was annoyed and turned to him and said, "Don't be videotaping me.
It's 3:00 in the morning, you should be videotaping women, you faggot. You must be a fag—"

He caught himself, and then he turned around and looked at
me. I said, "I'm not a faggot, so you're not hurting me, but you sound
really stupid talking like that. If one person gets a video of you talking like that, you could fuck up your legacy."

In that moment, he said, "I'm not ever going to use the 'faggot'
word again, but you don't need to use the word 'nigga' around me,
because I don't use that word either."

I said, "Okay, cool." That was our pact; he has never used it since.

***

179

One time, Floyd and I were chilling and I saw that he was looking at my watch. I had this cheap ass name brand watch on, and finally he asked, "What's that?"

I said, "That's Michael Kors."

He laughed and said, "No, that ain't Michael Kors. That's some other shit. A man's watch is his Bentley in the club, so your watch should reflect the type of clientele or type of people you're around. It's a conversation piece. It's not for decoration."

Then he went to his collection of watches and pulled one out. "Here man. Start the conversation with this." It had more diamonds than I could count in one glance. I appreciated the offer, and I was so excited that he offered me such an expensive gift, but I turned it down.

"I'm not going to accept your watch, because I want to be able to make enough money to buy you a watch." It was really important to me that he knew that I valued our relationship and that it had nothing to do with money. I saw how generous he was. People would come up to him needing their teeth fixed, needing help buying a new car, and he would throw them the money without hesitation. I'm not going to say they were using him, because he's very smart, but he would tell me how he would wake up every day to 400 text messages with at least half of them being people asking for money. It was really important from the very beginning that he knew I wasn't there for the money.

I threw the Michael Kors watch in the trash, and I left it at that.

After that, Floyd never offered anything for the next couple of years. I never asked for anything, but I was following him around, studying him, and learning him. I was absorbing all of the eight-hour/six-hour conversations.

***

One day, I was at the Lakers game and his daughter called me crying. I was on a date, and she told me about how she had a terrible situation at school and that the video was all over the internet. "Can you help me take it down? My mom said you work on the internet."

I said, "Yeah, not a problem." I called around, and I got it taken off all the sites. I left it at that.

About three months later, I was in Miami. I was in my room at the Fontainebleau while on vacation with Floyd and The Money Team. I brought a friend along with me, and we'd been there for about two weeks. I was surrounded by money, glitz, and glamour, but I had a real moment. I turned to my friend and said, "I don't know how I'm going to pay my rent. I ain't been working."

I'd spent a lot of my time with Floyd and The Money Team as an unofficial intern, but the money I was making back home was only paying minimum bills. I wasn't making the type of money that I was used to making because I wanted to work with Floyd full-time.

At some point during the vacation, Floyd called me down to the car which he had just retrieved from valet.

I came down, and he was sitting in a Rolls-Royce with his driver, Bruce. I get in the car, and shut the door. If you've ever been in a Rolls-Royce, once you shut the door, it's air-tight. It's noise proof.

We were sitting there, and he asked, "When that bullshit went down with my daughter, you took that off the internet?" I told him that I did.

Then he said, "You never asked me for no money or for nothing."

I said, "Nah, it wasn't about that. You guys are family."

He had a curious look on his face. "Yeah? You know what? In my life, rarely do my friends become family. The fact that you looked out for my daughter like that, and you didn't even ask me for nothing shows that you really care about me."

I said, "Of course I care about you."

He took $20,000 out of his bag and threw it in the back seat. He declared, "You never have to worry about money again. Just focus on building your brand." I could have broken down right then and there. How was this possible? After that, he supported everything that I did. He gave me a monthly budget to build my show and has been a big financial supporter by buying advertising space and sponsoring our show. It's the type of thing Rodney would have done if he was alive and had the money, for sure. Having that financial backing was great, but it was more important for us to have a genuine relationship. I will never be healed from losing Rodney, but I was grateful to have gained another brother that day.

14

CAREER REBRANDING

I LEFT EVERYTHING TO START HOLLYWOOD UNLOCKED from scratch with no promise of anything. I had to really focus on my business, and I felt it was time to have a real conversation with Lature about where we stood and where we were going. I was in love with him, but I didn't think he felt the same way. He was often selfish with his emotions and I felt that he didn't really have the capacity to love anything or anyone. As we were lying in bed one night, I asked him directly, "Are you in love with me?"

He had simply said, "No."

That was the defining moment when I had decided I was going to leave. I waited until we had some time together because he and I were both traveling. We had gone to the roof of our building and we were lying on the cabana when I presented my case:

"If you and I were in business together, and we invested everything we had into our business, but nothing we did worked and we weren't getting a return on our investment, what would we do? Would we stay in the business?"

He said, "No, we'd end the business." Then he looked at me. He caught on to what I was suggesting.

He tried to stop me, but I continued. "We can't stay in the relationship because it's comfortable, or because we're solid, or because we're stable; we have to separate ourselves to form our own paths to figure out our own level of independence and what really fulfills us."

For me, I felt like my passion was building Hollywood Unlocked and starting my own company. Lature had a dark cloud looming over his life because he had a toxic relationship with his father. His passions took him down another path, and he was involved in a few drug transactions with his father. He had his own stuff that he had to work through, and he ended up getting caught and going to prison.

When he left, he showed me that I had the courage to pursue what I needed because I felt like what I had wasn't enough. Even though he wasn't in love with me, our relationship taught me that I deserved to be loved. He showed me that I deserved someone trustworthy, honest, and loyal. I know that he genuinely cared about me.

Although we didn't work out, he was still one of the most genuine people I'd ever dated. There were other people I dated who only wanted to stay in the relationship because there are so many perks that come along with it. My lifestyle is very comfortable, and my circles seem impressive to other people. And once motherfuckers fly on a jet, I don't know what it does to them, but they want to do it all the time. I've come across countless people who want my lifestyle and I knew that they didn't really want me. That was the difference with Lature. Our connection was genuine and mutually fulfilling even though he ultimately wasn't the one for me.

***

As I continued to build my brand and make connections with dope people, I met Mona Scott-Young. I never think that it is by happenstance that people came into my life or that we were allowed to meet. I used to give everybody my phone number, or get everybody's phone number, and add a description of who they were. I always considered each new person valuable and so I tried my best to show that in my interactions. I knew that Mona had managed some major artists and I knew that she was also working as an executive on "Love & Hip Hop." I had gotten her number, and then when I was ready to get on the show, I just called her.

Then I got on "Love & Hip Hop," and I used my appearance there as a springboard. I ended my relationship, I called Mona, got on "Love & Hip Hop," and then that was it. I was excited to be on the show and I developed some long-lasting relationships with some of the people who were also on cast.

***

"Love & Hip Hop" was my introduction to the world, but my image on the show wasn't always one that reflected positively. On one episode, I had an argument with another cast member, Hazel E, and the entire "Love & Hip Hop" fan base witnessed me throw a drink in her face to conclude our conversation. After that incident, everyone had an opinion about who I was and why I did that. Some judged that I must have issues with women. I don't think I have issues with women in general, but I have had issues with individual women. Not because of their gender, but more because we clashed as people. I don't see a woman and go, "Oh, she reminds me of my mom," or, "Oh, she reminds me of my ex-girlfriend." I just think men handle conflict differently. Where I'm from, men will either call somebody from a gang or somebody from the streets to come holler at me, call me directly, or they'll pull up. Women do a lot of behind your back, shady, social media shade—it's more public, so people see that more. I'm not one to run from any conflict, so whether you're a woman or a man or whatever, I just feel like, shit, if you can dish it out, I can dish it out, too. I can guarantee that I hit harder.

Most people don't really know who I am beyond the veil of Hollywood Unlocked because I've purposely built that barrier. There aren't any photos of my family on Instagram or on Facebook. There aren't photos of who I'm in intimate relationships with, nor am I public about those relationships. Those people who share in that intimate space understand that. I don't broadcast my vulnerabilities or insecurities on Instagram or any of the shows I've been on. When I first joined "Love & Hip Hop," my contract was clear: we could talk about anything but my intimate relationships. As a result, there were no scenes with me being intimate with anyone or anything that alluded to a romantic association. I was very guarded. I was still working through the walls I constructed after Rodney died. I also specified that I didn't want to discuss my sexuality. I had never had the conversation with my family—not that they didn't know or wonder—but I had never officially told them that I was gay.

That brings me back to the situation with Hazel E. We were going back and forth, just throwing low blows at each other. This was my first scene on "Love & Hip Hop;" there was no coaching, no guidance, or conversations about how the scenes go. None of that. We went on for a while and she told me that everybody should know that I was in a relationship with a popular male actor. It was true, but the person she was trying to bring into the conversation was not comfortable disclosing his sexuality. I thought it was grossly disrespectful of her. I don't live a gay lifestyle; I don't live a straight lifestyle. I just go where I want to go, and I do what I want to do. I'd never been harassed or bullied for being gay, so I didn't know what that felt like. In that moment she, was not only attacking me, but she was also attempting to "out" somebody else and expose him. He had nothing to do with whatever issue she had with me. She did this knowing that this was a large platform and that this moment would be witnessed by millions of people. She was threatening to take away my choice in how I presented my sexuality not only to the world, but also to my friends and family—I still hadn't had that conversation with them. This wasn't how I wanted them to find out about me. I felt blind-sighted. All sorts of emotions started to surface, and I was filled with untamable rage.

That rage had been inside of me for years, but I had learned how to handle it for the most part. I know how destructive my temper can be, and I didn't want to have another situation like the one that had occurred with Josh. I know what's at stake if I blackout and lose it, but none of that mattered during that altercation with Hazel E. Honestly, it didn't matter who was sitting in front of me that day. It could have been Lil' Fizz, it could have been Ray J, it could have been Omarion—it could've been anybody. If anybody else had sat on that couch and did what she did, it probably would have been worse.

From a viewer's perspective, it was uncalled for. It was crazy of me to have done that. I threw the drink at her, and when I realized that I had snapped, I was able to catch myself. That's when I got up and walked out because it came to me, *Fuck! I gotta get out of here.* Had I stayed and let that moment overtake me, I would have gone from zero to a thousand. The cast didn't really know me like that and neither did the production team. I'm sure it was a shock to them as well.

The world saw a completely different version of the argument. I had complained about Hazel E bringing up my sexuality, and so they edited those parts of the conversation. When that episode finally aired, people only saw us having an argument and me throwing the drink. I'm not justifying what I did, but I do think that people should know the context. People who I thought were in my corner turned their backs on me. I felt betrayed and misunderstood, and to make matters worse, that incident ruined the relationship in question and he never talked to me again.

A couple of years later, when Hazel was bashing dark-skinned women and homosexuals, the whole world hated her. Then people were celebrating me for throwing the drink, but they didn't understand that her homophobia and ignorance is why I threw the drink. I still took a lot of heat from it, and I felt like it really created a narrative about me that isn't consistent with the type of person I am. I do have a heart. I do care about people and have compassion. When people place themselves in situations to agitate or create a situation that becomes tense like that, I think we all have our responsibility to learn how to walk away or defuse the situation. I took responsibility for throwing the drink, of course, but her words were triggering. I can't let anyone else put me back in that space. I lost control in a very public way, but I try to find the silver lining in everything. I was able to see myself the way other people saw me. I was able to evaluate my actions and be more conscious of how I presented myself to the world.

After that, I got tens of thousands of complaints on social media. Before that day, I had never had strangers come to my Instagram or to my social media and specifically tell me what they thought about me. Ever. It was overwhelming to wake up and have 10,000 or more comments dragging me for that incident. The comments never stopped, and I was so overwhelmed that I shut down and isolated myself. I thought that my decision that day ruined everything I had worked for, and that possibility was depressing.

I was getting death threats every day, and for the first year, I wouldn't take club bookings because I was paranoid that people were going to kill or kidnap me. People would offer me five, 10, and 15,000 dollars to come to cities to party, and I refused all that money because I felt like they were trying to set me up. Moving forward, I had to learn how to make sure I was aware of my branding and how I was filming. Then I launched my podcast. It became a space for me to control my own narrative so that those familiar with my brand had an opportunity to experience me beyond the scope of edited reality TV.

Despite everything, I don't regret it. Had that not been aired, I wouldn't have become one of the most talked-about people on TV that season. I also wouldn't have appeared in three times more episodes the next season. They almost rewarded bad behavior. A lot of the buzz around my name did come from that incident, and unfortunately, we live in a society where people like that kind of crazy shit. Even though my lack of judgment came with some perks, I was upset because, for a long time, that scene was the only perception of who I was.

***

Despite navigating through a less than favorable interactions with castmates, I can say that during my tenure on "Love & Hip Hop" I gained one of the best friendships I've ever had. I had suffered the loss of so many important people in my life, and I really didn't know how to make friends with people. I was fine with making associates and building relationships that were business-related, but

Cardi drilled through all the walls I had put up and she holds a special place in my heart. First, I liked Cardi before she was an artist, and before she was on "Love & Hip Hop." I appreciated how real and raw she was. It was so refreshing to experience this fiery young woman who was hood and funny, yet so vibrant and carefree. She was herself and she was hilarious. Cardi knew who I was, and I knew who she was, but we didn't know each other

The day I finally met Cardi, I was at a party at Diddy's house in Los Angeles. She was in town doing a bunch of press interviews because she had just released "Bodak Yellow" the day before. Everyone was excited about it, and it was gaining momentum like crazy. Cardi's publicist built a connection to me through Hollywood Unlocked and had asked us to post about the song, and we did. I liked her Patientce, her publicist's, vibe, so we remained in contact. While I was at Diddy's, I reached out to Cardi's publicist and told her that they should come by. Diddy had just posted "Bodak Yellow," but I don't think he and Cardi had ever met. There were so many people at the party that when Cardi and her publicist finally arrived, security wouldn't let anybody else in. I immediately went into problem-solving mode, so I found Diddy's son, Justin, so that he could help me get them in. I didn't want to leave a bad first impression by inviting her to a party that she couldn't even access. Justin went outside, and we got her in the party. When I finally got a chance to talk to her when she got inside, I was met with a very different Cardi. She was more relaxed and low-key.

"Hello, Queen," I did a humorous bow when I greeted her.

"No, I'm not the queen," she corrected me. I appreciated how humble she was, and while she was on top of the world with her song's release, she still knew that she hadn't "arrived yet."

Justin and I escorted her over to Diddy and introduced them. We had made previous arrangements for Cardi to be featured on Hollywood Unlocked, and then she yelled, "Yo, I'm coming on your show tomorrow! I can't wait."

The next day, when Cardi arrived at the studio, she was wearing a saucy black leather bustier and ripped glittery jeans. Her hair was an intense red-orange color, and her nails were elaborately decorated with jewels. Her ensemble was a perfect reflection of her personally: bold and daring.

One of the first questions I asked her was what she was good at, and she immediately shot out, "I'm good at sucking dick!" The shock-factor was refreshing. She continued, "All the guys tell me that, and I ain't gone teach nobody my secrets."

Her energy was electric, and we couldn't help but be enthralled by her. She was completely candid and hilarious—she wasn't shy about answering questions and was transparent about some of the struggles she encountered while working in the entertainment industry. It was a great interview, and I fell in love with her personality and her spirit. Afterward, she followed Hollywood Unlocked and we remained in contact through social media. Then out of the blue, she DM'd me and said, "Call me."

I told her, "Well, I don't have your number."

Then she said, "Oh, I thought I gave it to you." She gave me her number and then we talked every day after that. Our friendship budded because she is a genuine person. I admire the light she brings into everybody's life, and I admire how connected she is to the people who matter to her. Sometimes I don't really understand my impact, value, or influence on people, and she reminds me of that. She asks my advice and opinion about personal matters, and she runs a lot of ideas and plans by me. And those times when I have an opportunity to mentor or help her in any type of way reminds me of those days when I would look after Tamica. The fact that Cardi trusts me with the most vulnerable parts of herself shows me that I'm valuable to her, and all my life, that's all I've ever wanted from the people who claimed to love me.

15

Breaking Barriers in my Own Lane

———

M Y CAREER WAS ON THE RISE, AND I was enjoying the fruits of Hollywood Unlocked, but I still felt like there was more that I wanted to do. I wanted a new challenge, and I wanted to do something that was out-the-box. During my time of searching, I had watched an interview with Oprah Winfrey where she talked about getting the part of Miss Sophia in *Color Purple*. She said that she wanted the part and did everything she could to be cast, but she initially was denied. Then she said that she started working out, and as she was running on the treadmill, she began to sing, "I surrender All." Then she asked, "Lord, what do you want from me?" That resonated with me. That was a question I had for myself. Then she said, "Just please guide me. Tell me what you'd like me to do," and so on.

She said as soon as she was done saying the prayer, she got a call from Steven Spielberg who said she got the part. I was inspired.

That interview with Oprah never escaped my mind. Shortly after, I was getting ready to interview Jenifer Lewis on Hollywood Unlocked, so I started reading her book, *The Mother of Black Holly-wood*. I was reading a selection where she shares about having bipolar disorder, and I was going through a depression because of social media. Because of the content of Jenifer's book, I was excited about the interview.

While preparing for the interview, I spent a weekend in Ha-waii. I was going to read Jenifer Lewis's book while I was there, and it was a much-needed vacation. I had also gone there to relax with someone I was dating. While reading the book, I zeroed in on the part where she says she was on a cruise by herself and went out on the deck and said, "God, please send me a sign or something that this is meant for me—that I shouldn't walk away from the business."

Basically, she was ready to give up, and when she got back from vacation, her agent called and said, "You got 'Blackish.'" I was sitting there trying to explain to my date how much I was inspired, and he ended up taking a nap. I frowned and said, "Okay, I'm going to go out there and try it myself."

I went out onto the balcony, and I mustered up the courage to kick it with God.

I said, "Nigga (this is literally how I was talking to God), this is corny, but I'm going to try it. I know 'Love & Hip Hop' didn't work out for me. People didn't see me for who I am. Please, I want to get back on television because I want to show people that I'm more than the narrative that's been created by the show. Send me a sign, please. Alright."

I really did it as a joke, but, I swear to God, I came back, I landed after five and a half hours of flying over the water with no WiFi, and the only text message I had was from Nick Cannon saying, "Are you ready?"

When I called him, he said, "I'm going to hire you for 'Wild 'N Out.' Get ready." I agreed and he sent me a contract. It was a green light from that point on. The show really helped me reveal a different side of me: the fans were able to see me in a comedic sense, and whereas I never shared my sexuality on Love & Hip Hop, I was able to actually make all of my jokes about being gay. It was the different out-the-box experience I was longing for, and I was grateful to share in that space.

For my first episode, I booked Matt Barnes. I called him like, "Yo, you're in New York, and I know they been trying to book you for a couple of seasons. It would really make me look good to Nick and to the network if you can come and do the show. You'll be on the opposite team, so I'm going to prepare to come after you."

He agreed, so we booked him. I knew the games we were going to play with him, so I knew what I was going to do. I had an idea of the angles I was going to come from; I was going to be wild and do whatever.

Right before the taping, somebody close to Nick Cannon came to me and said, "Hey, I want to give you a heads-up: one of the producers doesn't believe that you should be here. They don't believe that you're comedic, and they just feel like you shouldn't be on the show. They switched Matt to be on your team."

I was completely thrown off because I didn't plan for Matt to be on my team. I was going to cheat because I knew Matt personally. I knew a lot of his business, and based on the games we would be playing, I knew there was shit I could do.

I went to the producer and said, "Hey, why did you guys switch Matt? I just booked him."

The producer said, "This is TV. It is what it is. You can figure it out."

I went over to Timothy DeLaGhetto, one of the other cast members, and said, "Hey, give me that bottle of Hennessy." I took the bottle to the face, and thought, *Fuck it. I'm going to get drunk, and I'm going to go out there and just talk shit.*

The first game we played was called "Plead the Fifth." When it was my turn, I went out there and said, "Hey, Nick, you brought me on the show. Thank you so much for giving me this opportunity. You know I don't rap, sing, or dance. I'm not a comedian. I mean, I'm funny and I talk shit, but more importantly, you showed me that, because I asked for the opportunity, you gave it to me. I'm really thankful for that."

Everybody started clapping, and I continued with the punchline, "But I forgot to ask you one more thing when you were on my show."

He said, "What's that?"

Me: "Can I suck your dick?"

The place went crazy. All the cast ran off stage, the whole audience was out of their seats, and people were on the ground. Nick couldn't even bring the show back together because everyone kept laughing and carrying on. Everyone on the stage was in complete shock.

Nick had a sucker in his mouth, and I wasn't done. I said, "Nick!" When he turned around, I took the sucker out his mouth, and I put it in my mouth. They fell out again.

That antic solidified my part on the show. The executives came out, and when I saw the white people come out the booth, I thought I was in trouble. They were amazed at how bold I was, and they expressed how they had never seen anything like it on the show. They said they appreciated how fearless and funny I was.

Despite putting all my effort into the episode, it never aired. I think my jokes were a little too risqué considering that "Wild 'N Out" is a family show. It didn't discourage me though. A few episodes later, I kissed Bobby Lytes, and it was the first time two guys had ever kissed on "Wild 'N Out" and on MTV. We even won a VMA for it. I appreciated my role on the show because I was afforded the opportunity to use that platform to break barriers and to have purpose. I came onto the show as an openly gay man and my goal was to normalize what America really looked like to the cast. When I first got there, I was told that there were some cast members who were homophobic and weren't comfortable with the gay jokes; I was able to come in and normalize making jokes with and about me, and it was okay for me to make jokes to, with, and about them, too. I believe that my presence made the audience look at the show in a very different way. They didn't have that dynamic on any other comedy show, so I'd like to take credit for the fact that we helped transform the show into becoming more aligned with America today.

My "Wild 'N Out" experience is also surreal to me because I remember wanting to be on MTV and wanting to go to the MTV Awards but being denied access. Now I am regularly on the network and have been on other major networks as well. It just reminded me that my hustle never stops. It never gets easier no matter where I am, and I have to keep going. My drive and determination put me in a position to create my own awards show where I have the final say in who's honored who's invited. "Wild 'N Out" pushed me to be really creative and continue to fight for bigger dreams.

iHeart

One of those bigger dreams was to partner with iHeart Radio to make Hollywood Unlocked a nationally syndicated show. I had been pitching my show to iHeart for a couple of years with no luck. Then I did an interview on The Breakfast Club and afterward Charlamagne said, "You need to come over to iHeart."

I said, "I know! I've been trying to for the last couple of years. I have a dinner tonight with Marissa Morris, the senior vice president." I had met Marissa in Cardi B's dressing room at one of the iHeart events in LA. At first I didn't know her or what she did; we just sparked up a conversation and she was super cool. We exchanged information, and she texted me her vCard; I saw that she was the senior vice president at iHeart. *Okay, great*, I thought. *I'm going to keep in touch with her.*

"Okay," Charlamagne went on, "but I'm going to text Doc Wynter. He's the senior vice president over urban programming. I'm going to tell him, too." He texted Doc Wynter just like he said.

I had dinner already scheduled that night after The Breakfast Club, and when I got there Marissa and I were talking. Then Tom Poleman, the chief programming officer and president of iHeart, walked in. Marissa introduced him to me, I followed up and sent some information about my show.

A couple of days later, I was on a phone call with Doc Wynter and Jennifer Leimgruber from Premiere Networks. We were discussing my brand, my vision, and what I wanted to do. I had always envisioned my brand existing in every vertical it could; I just didn't see iHeart as being the home for it. They started talking to me about syndicated radio and asking me if I would be open to it. Then a couple of months later, we had a deal. The first week I launched in 52 markets.

I had reached a career milestone for sure, and I felt like I was blazing a new trail in my industry. When Steve Harvey first syndicated, he was in three markets. The Breakfast Club was in eight markets. Big Boy is syndicated in about 13 or so markets. To launch in 52 markets right out the gate was huge. Also, even though I have a great opportunity with iHeart, I don't work for them. Some of what I gleaned from Floyd through his mentorship is that ownership is important. I have a partnership with them where I own the IP, the name, the podcast and the digital output. They own what airs on their network. It's a partnership where we split revenue and we work collaboratively.

***

Even though things were working out great for me with my career, I felt like there was an aspect of myself that people didn't understand. I still felt misjudged and it started to weigh on me. A defining moment for me was the day I met Rihanna at Fashion Week. A year and a half prior, Danyelle Crawley, who works with Nick Cannon on "Wild 'N Out," was telling me how much Rihanna wanted to meet me. I didn't believe that; I didn't think there was any way in hell that Rihanna even knew who I was. I don't assume that because I'm on TV, Instagram, or Hollywood Unlocked that somebody knows who I am. She didn't even remember that she had already met me at the RocNation brunch some years back when I was just starting out.

I went to Rihanna's party, and when we saw each other, she was really excited to see me, much to my surprise. Then she told me that she'd been wanting to meet me for a while. I was so amazed by that, but I didn't know why she wanted to meet me. I've done a really good job not allowing people to know who I am and allowing Hollywood Unlocked to be the façade, but Rihanna told me something that was so impactful, and I can't fully express how much it means to me:

"You know, I've been watching you for a while, and I feel bad when you get attacked. I can tell, deep down, you have a heart."

I wrinkled my forehead and said, "Really?"

She went on. "Yeah. I can also say that I know it's hard for you, having the job you have, to make friends with people who do what I do. But as a businesswoman, I respect how you built your brand."

That was significant, and I was blown away at the fact that she had paid that much attention to the trajectory of my career. Rihanna has over 74 million followers—I wouldn't have ever expected her to be watching me or dialed in to what I was doing. I thought that was pretty amazing, so after that, I talked about my experience meeting her on my show. I said, "You never know if somebody's going to measure up to what you expect them to be when you meet them. Rihanna exceeded that. If I never meet her again, I'm good because I had a good moment with her."

The next day, I got a call from someone who told me that Rihanna was having another party at Up & Down and that I should come by. When my friends and I arrived, some of Rihanna's people took me downstairs and escorted me to her table. When she saw me, she got excited all over again.

She yelled, "Oh, my God! Two days in a row! It's so good to see you again!"

In the midst of my hug and kiss, she said, "Another thing I forgot to tell you is that I was really sad when I heard you tell the story of how your brother got killed on 'Love & Hip Hop.'"

I wasn't even ready for her to say that. It wasn't a comment about my business, it was sympathy about something that affected me on a personal level. It was validating that someone on her level knew and was affected by my brother's story. One of the reasons why I went back to the show was to work through his death with my family and closest friends and to be open about the impact of Rodney's death. She cared. I can't really describe the impact, but oftentimes, people see me as some*thing*, but it was like Rihanna was seeing me as some*one*. She didn't see me as a "fill in the blank," she simply saw *me*. Her validation meant so much to me because in my journey, I'm constantly figuring out how to find value in myself.

16

BROKEN FAMILY TIES

―――――

THE OLDER I BECAME, THE LESS involved I was with my family. I'm very private and protective of my personal life, especially since I've become a notable person. I'm very isolated, but a lot of that came from being rejected by my father when I reached out to them after my brother, Rodney, died. I was trying to get all my brothers and sisters on the same page, but none of them really would do it. Everybody had their own shit, so I said, "Fuck them all." I stopped hanging with all of them. I stopped talking with all of them. I stopped going to functions. I didn't go to family reunions. I didn't come around to any of that. I isolated myself and started giving less of myself to them.

When my uncle passed away, I went home to attend the funeral, but I actually wondered if I would need to bring security. In a normal family, I don't know if anyone would think they'd need security around their loved ones, but that's how distant I am from my family. They're still trying to figure out what happened, but the truth is that for years I fought so hard for us to come together and be a family, and then I realized that I needed to just focus on me. That became the theme.

Holidays lose their warmth and charm when you don't have a connection with your family. When my dad turned 71 on the fifth of February, I didn't even call him. I don't feel what other people feel when it comes to Christmas and Thanksgiving with family. Those cheesy commercials with families in matching pajamas or sitting around the table exchanging smiles is not a part of my reality.

One time, my closest cousin Anthony called me out on my antisocial disposition toward my family. Anthony called me and said, "The family just doesn't understand why you don't fuck with them. Like they don't get it, you know? I tried to explain to them that you don't fuck with nobody."

"Shit, that's the truth," I admitted.

"You know, our cousins who grew up with us just don't understand why I'm the only one you bring around."

I don't trust anybody. I really feel like if I can control my world, I can control my peace. I can control my happiness. I can control not being betrayed.

***

Years later I was going through one of my moments when I was sad and having a hard time with Rodney's death, so I decided to reach out to my nephew, Roderick. His mother named him after my brother. I sent him a message on Facebook, and we started talking. He added me as a friend, and I was excited—he's my nephew and my brother's son so I was glad that I was able to still have some piece of Rodney. My nephew and I were discussing my brother, and he was telling me how much he remembered him, and we spent time reminiscing and such. After our exchange back and forth, I called my brother, Link, very optimistic and excited to tell him all about this connection I made with our nephew.

"Rodney's son found me on Facebook, and I really needed that. Talking to him has been great, and I'm going to meet up with him. I'm about to fly out to Stockton so that we can build a relationship."

Link stopped me swiftly and said, "That's not his son. Rodney just named him after him and treated him like his son. But that's not his son." He continued to tell me all about Roderick's real dad, and I was devastated. I felt like Rodney was slipping away from me, and finding out that Roderick wasn't his destroyed me. Then I was angry at how insensitive my brother was in telling me. Then, to know how much I loved my brother and how excited I was that I had made this connection with a part of him and to tell me that way, I was angry. Apparently, everybody knew but me, so I felt like I was the butt of a horrible joke.

I called Roderick back, and I guess you could say that I confronted him.

"Roderick, I gotta ask you a question. I just talked to my brother and he says that you're not Rodney's son."

Roderick was as quiet as a mouse pissing on cotton. When he finally spoke he said, "Well, Rodney is the dad that I know. Rodney's the guy that raised me as a kid. Rodney is my dad, but not my biological dad." Then my devastation reached a new height. I was so overwhelmed that I hung up the phone.

Afterward, Roderick texted his mom and told her, "I think you should call Jason because he didn't know Rodney wasn't my dad, and now he's emotional."

She called me and we had a very emotional conversation. I explained to her how confused I was and how distressing the whole situation was. After all that, I still decided to maintain a relationship with Roderick. We still talk, and we had a heartfelt conversation where he told me that he wanted to maintain a relationship with me and that it was important to him. I understood. I keep in touch with him because Rodney would've wanted us to have a relationship because Rodney treated him like he was his son. It was still a hard truth to digest, but like everything else that pertains to Rodney, I have to learn how to heal past it.

Despite my initial disappointment about Roderick, I had never forgotten about Mytae, Rodney's biological daughter. She was seven weeks old when he was killed, and we didn't reconnect until she was an adult. I wish that I could have been there to help raise her, but there was a lot of drama stopping that. My brother was a Blood, but Mytae's mom had gotten involved with a Crip after my brother died.

To make matters worse, this was someone who my brother didn't like and really didn't fuck with. After she got into a relationship with him, she changed Mytae's last name from Townsend, my brother's last name, to her boyfriend's last name. Everybody in our city knew that his family, and nobody fucked with them. To put his name on her like that was so disrespectful to us and to Rodney.

When I saw that her last name on Facebook had changed, I messaged her and said, "This is really disrespectful. This is the most disrespectful shit I've ever seen." At that time, she didn't have a relationship with me, so it was really random of me to send her that.

She retorted, "That's the only dad I knew growing up."

I couldn't get past it. I told her, "I understand he's the only guy you knew growing up as your dad. But you don't understand the history enough to understand how disrespectful that is." Her mom ended up calling me, and I went off on her. It was hard to have a relationship with my niece after that because I didn't know where to go from there.

Eventually, I realized how rude I was for attacking her. Rodney is always a sore spot for me, but Mytae had no control over Rodney's death, the preservation of his memory, or who raised her. She had nothing to do with the beefs—past or present. My goal was to reach out to her and let her know that I understand the position she was in and that she's not responsible for my feelings.

***

While I was filming season six of "Love & Hip Hop," I went home to plan a memorial for Rodney. I had met with my siblings so that we could discuss details, but my brother, Link, acted like a complete ass and stormed out—because his wife was in the scene. In many ways, he's become my father, but that's probably because he actually had a relationship with my father. The man tucked him in every night. He has kids out of his marriage, like my father and he had no regard for anyone else—like my father. He got upset with me because I mentioned how shitty of a parent our father was. I was the only kid who went to foster care and was there for years. Not to mention, I was raising my goddamn self before then because he didn't step up when my mother checked out. He didn't understand where I was coming from, or how I felt—none of them could really understand my perspective because none of them were in my shoes. Not to mention, Link was the one who got me shot, and he didn't even apologize for it.

He was huffing and puffing talking about, "Ain't nobody gonna disrespect my father," and that turned the entire meeting into something it didn't have to be. We were there for Rodney; how could we honor him if we couldn't even honor each other?

My father didn't even show up to the meeting, even though I called and told him that I wanted to talk to him. After the big blow-up with Link, I called my dad to schedule a time to meet with him, and he blew me off. That was the last straw, and so I'm over trying to rebuild that relationship. Now I just have to live for myself, and put that energy into people who deserve it.

When we taped the memorial for Rodney on "Love & Hip Hop," Mytae was there. She spoke about Rodney, and about not having the privilege of knowing him and that he must've been a great person because she's heard so many great stories. She was just seemed grateful to be there and to have started a relationship with all of us. It was the first time she had really been around that side of the family and the first time that she had ever spoken publicly about her father. Afterward, we released 27 white doves to symbolize the age Rodney was when he was murdered. Mytae and I didn't have a chance to sit down and build a relationship while filming the show, but I did take her to meet Cardi B because I knew she was a fan. The relationship is slowly progressing. Rodney would've expected us all to have a relationship anyway. He's such an important part of my life that I think it would be disingenuous for me to say how important he is to me and then not be there to have a relationship with his daughter.

***

The concept of "family" had always been fluid to me. Some of the people who I considered family as a kid or teenager don't really hold that title now, but some do. The people who I regard as permanent family and have really had my back like the closest brothers and sisters are Calvin and Floyd. Calvin has seen the worst of me and still considers me redeemable. He's forgiving, supportive, and real— I value where our time together has brought us. I get a lot of criticism for always talking about Floyd, but how do I not honor someone who's been such a big influence in my life? He's someone who helped me realize my potential, and he put his money, his brand, and his full support behind me. He brought me into The Money Team and into his world. I was living in Hollywood and knowing everybody, but not feeling connected to anybody—and I got pulled into Floyd's family. He's family, even with our ups and downs.

Then there are Tiffany Haddish, Queen Latifah, and Cardi B. These are people who are the top of the industry, but I don't view them as celebrities. When I speak to Tiffany, there's always a reaffirmation of my purpose from her, a supporting comment, or encouragement. She always tells me that she believes in me and that I'm going to be huge in this industry. Queen Latifah has always been a big sister to me and took a chance on a smart-mouthed kid from Stockton. She was the light that I never had. Her validating me and showing me love really inspired me to believe in myself. I attribute a lot of my survival after Rodney's death to her.

And again, Cardi. I tell her things that I can't tell anybody else, and she gives me that same exclusivity. My extended family is there and they take my calls whenever I need to talk to them about something. We go beyond industry shit and just support each other in life. They're also people who understand the importance of maintaining privacy, so they know I'm going to maintain their privacy. I know I can trust them with anything; I know they're going to maintain mine, too.

It's amazing to me how I grew up with so many tarnished relationships within my family, but God allowed me to be in a space where I could regain what was lost. I never look to my friends to be replacements for anyone, but it sure helps to have them when I feel like I have nobody else.

I Am Not an Anomaly

O ne of the many lessons that Floyd taught me was that the bad guy
always wins. He was right. One of the most disappointing parts
about my industry is that a lot of the conflict I've created with my
business has actually been great *for* my business. If I drop a story that
says that Janet Jackson is pregnant at 50, people would have a lackluster response, but if I drop a story revealing someone's mistress or
secret baby mama, the energy and momentum surrounding that story
would be through the roof. There's not enough material in a day for
the amount of scandal and negativity people want to consume, but
this is an indictment on the world that we live in, not on me.

Even though playing dirty has worked out for my business, it's
been a challenge separating my business from my personal brand. I've
been painted as "the bad guy," and I think that it's hard for people
to see past that. When people have an opportunity to meet me, they
say things like, "Man, you're nothing like what people think," or,

"You're way nicer than people think," or, "Goddamn, you're not as messy as people think."

Despite people's opinions of me, I can honestly say that I'm finally living out my dream of being a self-made entrepreneur in the entertainment industry. I've been able to continually focus on building an audience that will help me eventually have a platform to inspire, motivate, and help people. I've partnered with iHeartRadio, and my show is accessible to 52 markets across the country. I'm excited to do the talk show circuit, and I'm glad that even though I initially walked away from "Love & Hip Hop" after two seasons, I was able to solidify a place on "Wild 'N Out" and then come back to "Love & Hip Hop" on my terms. I got everything I wanted contractually, monetarily, and I was able to take charge of my own story. I've gotten to a point in my career where now I can say, "Yo, I'm signing with ICM, one of the biggest agencies in the world," and I'm able to do all of this my way.

People's opinions or what they have to say about what I do don't matter to me. I've been molested and abandoned. I endured a lot, and I have lost much, yet I took all the obstacles and darts that have been thrown at me and crafted them into a throne. I've grieved until I've become physically ill due to my brother's death and the deaths of other people I cared about. Once I experienced Rodney's death, I knew that there was nothing that could reproduce that type of pain. Having known that pain, nothing anybody says or does can move me. I've already had the worst happen to me and I survived it. If I lose a contract, it's not a problem; I'll go find another one. If I lose a friend, I'd be sad because I don't just throw around that label, but I just see it as God closing that chapter. I keep it moving. I've learned that no matter what happens to me and what I face, God's favor is on my life.

My life is a testament of faith. For a while, I thought that God had turned his back on me. I thought that I was too far gone or that I had done too much dirt for him to be invested in my life. I was wrong. He had never left me, and he has been evident in my darkest days and my brightest moments. Even though I had absentee parents, God still gave me great mentors like the Easters, Edwin, Dana ... Rodney. Even though I was in the foster care system, I learned survival. I learned how to stand up for myself and how to assert myself in any situation. I lost my brother, but it fueled me to make a change in my life and pursue my dreams. It grounded me and forced me to feel every emotion and experience. With each test, I was able to endure and just ask, "What's next?" At first, I thought it was just because I was numb from pain, but now I know it's from having strength and understanding that God is going to see me through.

I am not an anomaly. God is using every experience to propel you to your destiny, but you can't fold and give up. Every debilitating event or earth-shattering loss is equipping you for something inconceivably vast. It doesn't matter what your background is, what mistakes you've made, or what demons you have to fight—continue to push knowing that you have what it takes to be grand. What God did for me, he can also do for you. I lay waste to every feeling of hopelessness, suicide, low-self-esteem, unworthiness, shame, guilt, and oppression. You are not the sum of your mistakes or your misfortune; rather, you are an opportunity for God's glory. Just as God's hand was on me throughout my life, I assure you that his hand is on you, too. One thing my life has taught me is that God never forgot about me, and he hasn't forgotten about you either.

JASON LEE

Culture disruptor and media mogul, Jason Lee, has unlocked the secret to true success in Hollywood. Lee has built an ever-evolving brand empire through strategic campaign oversight, event production, and influencer relationships. Not only has Lee been at the forefront of culture shifting moments, but includes an expansive clientele of notable celebrities and personalities including Chris Brown, Jordin Sparks, Kris Jenner, Rob Kardashian, and Jamie Foxx. Lee's executed various campaigns for brands such as T-Mobile, Samsung, Belaire, Monster Headphones, Fashion Nova, Men's US National Soccer Team, Audi, 2Vllve and Quarterly.

When Lee is not executing global brand campaigns, he's building a world class leading media platform. Hollywood Unlocked is one of the nation's Top 5 Urban & entertainment brands and is notably referenced as the pulse of pop culture. As editor-in-chief of Holly-wood Unlocked, Lee delivers fast-breaking, social buzzing-entertain-ment interviews and coverage around the clock.

Since its inception in 2015, Hollywood Unlocked can be found in the nation's top news and entertainment shows such as: The Real, Wendy Williams, NY Post, Complex, MSNBC, NPR, Us Weekly, Vanity Fair and more. The millennial audience-driven platform con-tinues to produce thousands of hours of content and drives engage-ment of over 550 million impressions per month. The radio subsid-iary of Hollywood Unlocked, Hollywood Unlocked Uncensored, is feeding the eager demands of today's consumers about its favorite celebrities, it's also creating unforgettable trending moments with star guests such as Cardi B, Amber Rose, Abby Lee Miller, Nick Cannon and more. In an ever-evolving journalism industry, Holly-wood Unlocked also totes a strategic media partnership with unde-feated boxing champion, Floyd Mayweather.

In the competitive world of entertainment, Lee has elevated his brand recognition as a pivotal voice on the VH1 show "Love & Hip Hop Hollywood" and the fresh new personality on MTV2's "Wild N' Out." It's all in the numbers, as Lee's influence reaches over 7 million dedicated viewers each week. Lee continues to shine as the talent and face of the Hollywood Unlocked brand. Media Strategist, Entrepreneur, and Thought Leader...Jason Lee is just getting started.

Made in the USA
Middletown, DE
08 February 2024

49315173R00135